Politicuffs

*There's Nothing Patriotic
About Political Ignorance*

Keith Berkner

authorHOUSE®

AuthorHouse™
1663 Liberty Drive
Bloomington, IN 47403
www.authorhouse.com
Phone: 1 (800) 839-8640

Published by AuthorHouse   03/16/2016

ISBN: 978-1-5049-6435-7 (sc)
ISBN: 978-1-5049-6433-3 (hc)
ISBN: 978-1-5049-6434-0 (e)

Library of Congress Control Number: 2015920050

Print information available on the last page.

Welcome

There is absolutely nothing patriotic about political ignorance!

When critics of Barack Obama tell you that this is now Barack Obama's economy, and no longer George W Bush's economy, they make it sound as if they are waiting for you to explain away the performance numbers under Obama's presidency.

Quite the contrary, every Democrat on God's green earth should pee their pants in excitement for the opportunity to engage the critics in that conversation.

When they make the statement that "it is now Obama's economy," understand that what they really mean is that they do not want you to remind them of the baselines that Barack Obama inherited from George W Bush.

Nonetheless, this is *exactly* the mentality that you want to encounter in a political debate, as it gives you an opening to not only defend the success of President Obama's policies and the Democratic party, but it allows you a chance to educate your political opponents on the definitive data, the historical baselines, and the proper perspectives.

After years of debating politics, I have found that there are five major mistakes that people make when discussing the issues:

- Not knowing basic economic baseline data

    This includes:
    - GDP
    - Job creation data
    - Unemployment rates
    - Labor participation rates
    - The reasons why "93 million Americans are out of the workforce' (actually it's more)
    - Deficits
    - National Debt

- Not understanding any real historical perspectives on the economic data
- Not understanding when fiscal years begin and end
- Not understanding that FY 2009 was George W Bush's final fiscal year – and not Barack Obama's first fiscal year
- Not understanding basic perspectives on American foreign policy

Before we begin, I simply cannot stress *enough* that FY 2009 is *the* elephant in the room and is *critical* to understand for virtually any political discussion involving George W Bush and Barack Obama. This simply cannot be overstated. Keep that in mind going forward.

Though the economic baseline data aforementioned may seem intimidating at first, I have tried to format this book in a simple yet effective manner.

Foreword

He who knows the data wins the debate.

Unfortunately, America's television media seem all too concerned with TV ratings, sensationalism, "shock journalism" and the entertainment factor to bother with educating its audiences in an intelligent manner, on the most significant political, economic and foreign policy issues of our day.

Seemingly, America's media would rather discuss false scandals and meaningless data measurements to keep their audiences stirred up, rather than give their audiences proper insight and definitive data and sources, for which they could use to either confirm, challenge or deny what they are being told.

Right-wing media, in particular, seem to thrive on fake scandals. In the early days of Obama's presidency, it was Jeremiah Wright, ACORN, and Obama's birth certificate. More recently, the "scandals" have evolved around emails, golf rounds, vacations, and my very favorite – Benghazi!

When the news has been good, the right-wing of the Republican Party has preferred to either challenge the credibility of the news source, or ignore the message altogether. Many times, the GOP has changed its standards of measurement once the previous standards of measurement have fallen by the wayside – and with it, the associated talking points.

Frankly, at times, Republicans remind me of six year-old kids who jump up and down with their hands over their ears refusing to believe anything other than "1 plus 1 equals 3," regardless of what evidence or perspective is presented to them.

Keith Berkner

This book's title, "Politicuffs," and its content, invoke an *aggressive* tone by design. This book is a tool that will give Democrats the ammunition to take on Republican rhetoric in a tough, but thought-provoking and effective manner.

For Republicans, this book should challenge the premises of your party's platform and long-time held beliefs and policies, by using basic analysis of historical data.

I hope you enjoy the ride.

Table of Contents

Themes of "Politicuffs"

> ➢ Perspective is the Great Equalizer.

> ➢ There's Nothing Patriotic About Political Ignorance.

> ➢ He who knows the data wins the debate.

> ➢ "I don't want to see religious bigotry in any form. It would disturb me if there was a wedding between the religious fundamentalists and the political right. The hard right has no interest in religion except to manipulate it."[1]

> *- Reverend Billy Graham*

---

[1] Parade, February 1, 1981. Also cited in "Thy Kingdom Come: How the Religious Right Distorts Faith and Threatens America."

Gross Domestic Product

During the 2012 presidential campaign season, when Mitt Romney was asked how long a Romney administration should be given before it is judged on its performance, Romney replied, "6 to 12 months."[2]

Most economists would probably agree with Mitt Romney's response, as it generally takes that long for an incoming administration's policies to – pardon the expression – "trickle down" throughout the economy. Keep this in the back of your mind when you look at the data; in particular, GDP, jobs, and, of course, FY spending.

Though Quarterly GDP Data Tables for presidents going back to Jimmy Carter are provided, keep in mind that the *focus* of the GDP data in this book is primarily twofold.

> ➤ First, the GDP data is to show a distinction between where we were in FY 2008 and FY 2009, under George W Bush's final fiscal years, and where we are today.

> ➤ Second, GDP data *beyond* that objective is provided for the purpose of historical perspective, going back to January 1977.

What is GDP?

GDP, or Gross Domestic Product, is the value of goods and services produced by the nation's economy.[3] The Bureau of Economic Activity

[2] USNews.com; "Bill Clinton is Right: The Economy Really Does do Better Under Democrats;" September 6, 2012.
[3] BEA.gov.

(BEA) measures GDP. Current and historical GDP data are found online at BEA.gov. Throughout the book, references are given to specific Tables at BEA.gov for confirmation of data contained herein and as a source for future GDP data.

A Gradual Economic Recovery

Though the recovery from the Great Recession has indeed been gradual due to the recession's severe depth, one would swear that Obama's critics were comatose in 2008 and 2009. They seem to reflect back on the Bush years at times as if they were the "Golden Age." They seem to forget that economists were warning us on the *front* end of the recession, how long the economic recovery might take and how painful it might be.

When the critics tell you that this is now "Obama's economy," this is *exactly* what you *want* to hear, as it opens up the door for the informed to educate the uninformed. As an informed Democrat, don't be afraid when you hear this type of nonsense from your political opponents. This is exactly where it starts. This is exactly where you *want* it to start.

Setting the Standard for Debate

It is critical to understand some of the baselines, in order to evaluate Obama's performance with any sort of credibility. After all, how can one judge anyone's performance on *anything* if one does not understand what those baselines are?

FY 2009 provides a classic textbook example in the study of government that few other years in the history of our country can. In discussing President Obama's performance on the U.S. economy, it is essential to have an understanding of the economic activity (GDP) baseline. You do this by pointing out the economic baseline that George W Bush left Barack Obama.

On GDP, then, what is Obama's baseline?

GDP during 4th Quarter 2008 was -8.2% (**Table 6**).[4]

> ➤ This was the last full quarter that George W Bush was in office.

> ➤ Barack Obama began his presidency from this essential baseline.

****

To confirm the GDP percent changes:

> ➤ Go to BEA.gov

> ➤ Under U.S. Economic Accounts:

> ➤ Under "National," select Gross Domestic Product (GDP)

> ➤ Under Gross Domestic Product (GDP):

> ➤ Select "Percent change from preceding period"

When Republicans talk about a slow economic recovery under Barack Obama, this is *exactly* where you, as a Democrat, want the debate to begin – in the 4th Quarter of 2008 (**Table 1** or **Table 6**).

****

As **Table 1** below indicates, our economy contracted three of the last four quarters that George W Bush was in office. **Table 1** incorporates elements of Table 1.1.1. (Percent change from preceding period) and Table 1.1.5. (Current-dollar and "real" GDP), from the Bureau of Labor Statistics (BLS. gov).

---

[4] Bureau of Economic Activity (BEA.gov) as of 15 October 2015.

To confirm GDP in Dollars:

➢ Go to BEA.gov

➢ Under U.S. Economic Accounts:

➢ Under "National," select Gross Domestic Product (GDP)

➢ Under Gross Domestic Product (GDP):

➢ Select "Current-dollar and "real" GDP

In the 4ᵗʰ Quarter 2008, GDP was -8.2%.[5]

CY	Qtr	Increase (Decrease)	Billions of Dollars	FY	Qtr
2008	1	(2.7)	14,668.4	2008	2
2008	2	2.0	14,813.0	2008	3
2008	3	(1.9)	14,843.0	2008	4
2008	4	(8.2)	14,549.9	2009	1

Table 1

Despite what Obama critics would have you believe about our economy, current GDP stands in stark contrast to the -8.2% GDP when George W Bush left the White House.

CY	CY Qtr	Increase (Decrease)	Billions of Dollars	FY	FY Qtr
2014	3	4.3	17,522.1	2014	4
2014	4	2.1	17,615.9	2015	1
2015	1	0.6	17,649.3	2015	2
2015	2	3.9	17,902.0	2015	3
2015	3	1.5	18,034.8	2015	4

Table 2[6]

---

[5] BEA.gov. October 5, 2015. Table 1.1.1. (Percent Change from Preceding Period in Real Gross Domestic Product.) Table 1.1.5. (Gross Domestic Product (billions of dollars). Seasonally Adjusted at annual rates.)

[6] BEA.gov; Revision, as of 29 October 2015. Table 1.1.1. (Percent Change from Preceding Period in Real Gross Domestic Product.) Table 1.1.5. (Gross Domestic Product (billions of dollars) Seasonally Adjusted at annual rates.)

> Again, this is where you convey the message of the massive contraction (8.2%) in economic activity (GDP) that George W Bush left to Barack Obama (**table 1**).

> This is where you draw a significant and very important distinction between where we were as the Bush era ended and where we are now, under Barack Obama (**Table 1, Table 2, Table 6,** and **Table 7**).

At this point in the debate, you are up 1-0.

Remember – he who knows the data wins the debate.
Every time.

Note: All data from the following Tables reflect Quarterly GDP data taken from the Bureau of Economic Activity website (BEA.gov). Current as of October 29, 2015. FY 1977 was Gerald Ford's last fiscal year. Fiscal years begin October 1ˢᵗ of the year following inauguration into office.

Quarterly GDP
(1977 – 2015)

CY	Qtr	Increase (Decrease)	Billions of Dollars	FY	Qtr
1977	1	4.7	1992.5	1977	2
1977	2	8.1	2060.2	1977	3
1977	3	7.3	2122.4	1977	4
1977	4	0.0	2168.7	1978	1
1978	1	1.4	2208.7	1978	2
1978	2	16.5	2336.6	1978	3
1978	3	4.0	2398.4	1978	4
1978	4	5.5	2482.2	1979	1
1979	1	0.8	2531.6	1979	2
1979	2	0.5	2595.9	1979	3
1979	3	2.9	2670.4	1979	4
1979	4	1.0	2730.7	1980	1
1980	1	1.3	2796.5	1980	2
1980	2	(7.9)	2799.9	1980	3
1980	3	(0.6)	2860.0	1980	4
1980	4	7.6	2993.5	1981	1
1981	1	8.5	3131.8	1981	2
1981	2	(2.9)	3167.3	1981	3
1981	3	4.7	3261.2	1981	4
1981	4	(4.6)	3283.5	1982	1
1982	1	(6.5)	3273.8	1982	2
1982	2	2.2	3331.3	1982	3
1982	3	(1.4)	3367.1	1982	4
1982	4	0.4	3407.8	1983	1

Table 3

CY	Qtr	Increase (Decrease)	Billions of Dollars	FY	Qtr
1983	1	5.3	3480.3	1983	2
1983	2	9.4	3583.8	1983	3
1983	3	8.1	3692.3	1983	4
1983	4	8.5	3796.1	1984	1
1984	1	8.2	3912.8	1984	2
1984	2	7.2	4015.0	1984	3
1984	3	4.0	4087.4	1984	4
1984	4	3.2	4147.6	1985	1
1985	1	4.0	4237.0	1985	2
1985	2	3.7	4302.3	1985	3
1985	3	6.4	4394.6	1985	4
1985	4	3.0	4453.1	1986	1
1986	1	3.8	4516.3	1986	2
1986	2	1.9	4555.2	1986	3
1986	3	4.1	4619.6	1986	4
1986	4	2.1	4669.4	1987	1
1987	1	2.8	4736.2	1987	2
1987	2	4.6	4821.5	1987	3
1987	3	3.7	4900.5	1987	4
1987	4	6.8	5022.7	1988	1
1988	1	2.3	5090.6	1988	2
1988	2	5.4	5207.7	1988	3
1988	3	2.3	5299.7	1988	4
1988	4	5.4	5412.7	1989	1
1989	1	4.1	5527.4	1989	2
1989	2	3.2	5628.4	1989	3
1989	3	3.0	5711.6	1989	4
1989	4	0.9	5763.4	1990	1
1990	1	4.5	5890.8	1990	2
1990	2	1.6	5974.7	1990	3
1990	3	0.1	6029.5	1990	4
1990	4	(3.4)	6023.3	1991	1
1991	1	(1.9)	6054.9	1991	2
1991	2	3.1	6143.6	1991	3
1991	3	1.9	6218.4	1991	4
1991	4	1.8	6279.3	1992	1

Table 4

CY	Qtr	Increase (Decrease)	Billions of Dollars	FY	Qtr
1992	1	4.8	6380.8	1992	2
1992	2	4.5	6492.3	1992	3
1992	3	3.9	6586.5	1992	4
1992	4	4.1	6697.6	1993	1
1993	1	0.8	6748.2	1993	2
1993	2	2.4	6829.6	1993	3
1993	3	2.0	6904.2	1993	4
1993	4	5.4	7032.8	1994	1
1994	1	4.0	7136.3	1994	2
1994	2	5.6	7269.8	1994	3
1994	3	2.4	7352.3	1994	4
1994	4	4.6	7476.7	1995	1
1995	1	1.4	7545.3	1995	2
1995	2	1.4	7604.9	1995	3
1995	3	3.5	7706.5	1995	4
1995	4	2.9	7799.5	1996	1
1996	1	2.7	7893.1	1996	2
1996	2	7.2	8061.5	1996	3
1996	3	3.7	8159.0	1996	4
1996	4	4.3	8287.1	1997	1
1997	1	3.1	8402.1	1997	2
1997	2	6.2	8551.9	1997	3
1997	3	5.2	8691.8	1997	4
1997	4	3.1	8788.3	1998	1
1998	1	4.0	8889.7	1998	2
1998	2	3.9	8994.7	1998	3
1998	3	5.3	9146.5	1998	4
1998	4	6.7	9325.7	1999	1
1999	1	3.2	9447.1	1999	2
1999	2	3.3	9557.0	1999	3
1999	3	5.1	9712.3	1999	4
1999	4	7.1	9926.1	2000	1
2000	1	1.2	10,031.0	2000	2
2000	2	7.8	10.278.3	2000	3
2000	3	0.5	10,357.4	2000	4
2000	4	2.3	10,472.3	2001	1

Table 5

CY	Qtr	Increase (Decrease)	Billions of Dollars	FY	Qtr
2001	1	(1.1)	10,508.1	2001	2
2001	2	2.1	10,638.4	2001	3
2001	3	(1.3)	10,639.5	2001	4
2001	4	1.1	10,701.3	2002	1
2002	1	3.7	10,834.4	2002	2
2002	2	2.2	10,934.8	2002	3
2002	3	2.0	11,037.1	2002	4
2002	4	0.3	11,103.8	2003	1
2003	1	2.1	11,230.1	2003	2
2003	2	3.8	11,370.7	2003	3
2003	3	6.9	11,625.1	2003	4
2003	4	4.8	11,816.8	2004	1
2004	1	2.3	11,988.4	2004	2
2004	2	3.0	12,181.4	2004	3
2004	3	3.7	12,367.7	2004	4
2004	4	3.5	12,256.2	2005	1
2005	1	4.3	12,813.7	2005	2
2005	2	2.1	12,974.1	2005	3
2005	3	3.4	13,205.4	2005	4
2005	4	2.3	13,381.6	2006	1
2006	1	4.9	13,648.9	2006	2
2006	2	1.2	13,799.8	2006	3
2006	3	0.4	13,908.5	2006	4
2006	4	3.2	14,066.4	2007	1
2007	1	0.2	14,233.2	2007	2
2007	2	3.1	14,422.3	2007	3
2007	3	2.7	14,569.7	2007	4
2007	4	1.4	14,685.2	2008	1
2008	1	(2.7)	14,668.4	2008	2
2008	2	2.0	14,813.0	2008	3
2008	3	(1.9)	14,843.0	2008	4
2008	4	(8.2)	14,549.9	2009	1
2009	1	(5.4)	14,383.9	2009	2
2009	2	(0.5)	14,340.4	2009	3
2009	3	1.3	14,384.4	2009	4
2009	4	3.9	14,566.5	2010	1

Table 6

CY	CY Qtr	Increase (Decrease)	Billions of Dollars	FY	FY Qtr
2010	1	1.7	14,681.1	2010	2
2010	2	3.9	14,888.6	2010	3
2010	3	2.7	15,057.7	2010	4
2010	4	2.5	15,230.2	2011	1
2011	1	(1.5)	15238.4	2011	2
2011	2	2.9	15,460.9	2011	3
2011	3	0.8	15,587.1	2011	4
2011	4	4.6	15,785.3	2012	1
2012	1	2.7	15,973.9	2012	2
2012	2	1.9	16,121.9	2012	3
2012	3	0.5	16,227.9	2012	4
2012	4	0.1	16,297.3	2013	1
2013	1	1.9	16,440.7	2013	2
2013	2	1.1	16,526.8	2013	3
2013	3	3.0	16,727.5	2013	4
2013	4	3.8	16,957.6	2014	1
2014	1	(0.9)	16,984.3	2014	2
2014	2	4.6	17,270.0	2014	3
2014	3	4.3	17,522.1	2014	4
2014	4	2.1	17,615.9	2015	1
2015	1	0.6	17,649.3	2015	2
2015	2	3.9	17,913.7	2015	3
2015	3	1.5[7]	18,034.8	2015	4
2015	4			2016	1
2016	1			2016	2
2016	2			2016	3
2016	3			2016	4
2016	4			2017	1
2017	1			2017	2
2017	2			2017	3
2017	3			2017	4

Table 7

---

[7] BEA.gov, as of November 9, 2015.

Note

FY 1977 was Gerald Ford's last FY.

FYs 1978-1981 were Jimmy Carter's FYs.

FYs 1982-1989 were Ronald Reagan's FYs.

FYs 1990-1993 were George HW Bush's FYs.

FYs 1994-2001 were Bill Clinton's FYs.

FYs 2002-2009 were George W Bush's FYs.

FYs 2010-2017 are Barack Obama's FYs.

Job Creation

Republicans love to *claim* that they are the party of pro-job growth. Each election campaign cycle, seemingly every Republican seeking office reminds us of this. Yet, when we analyze the historical job creation data, nothing in the data supports that claim.

When it comes to job growth numbers and President Obama's performance, this is where it gets good. When it comes to analyzing whether GOP policies reflect historical realities, it gets real good.

If you have never looked at historical job creation data before, prepare yourself for an eye-opening experience. If you're a Democrat, you are in for a treat here. If you are a supply-sider Republican, this may be the point in which you question whether your party's ideology "shapes" its truisms to match its rhetoric.

Tables provided in the following pages indicate:

> ➤ Total number of jobs by President

> ➤ Average number of monthly jobs by President

> ➤ Total number of jobs by Party

> ➤ Job Market data 2008-2010

> ➤ Jobs by year by President

> ➤ Monthly average by President

Finally, perspectives are given which contrast the major differences in Republican vs. Democratic administrations. The perspectives given drive home the point of the absolute insanity of Republican claims that they are the pro job party.

Some Basics to Know

Going forward, keep in mind that the Bureau of Labor Statistics (BLS) calculates the Jobs data. New monthly job data is scheduled for release at 8:30 am on the first Friday of each month, for the preceding month and may be accessed at BLS.gov.

> ➢ **The Jobs data was taken from Bureau of Labor Statistics November 9, 2015 and includes data through October 2015. The job data used throughout "Politicuffs" includes the pending jobs data for September and October 2015.**

Total Number of Jobs by President8

Let's start with a basic analysis of just how contemporary presidents have fared in creating jobs, as this is probably the most basic and effective way of seeing the data. Keep in mind here that Republicans have strongly contended that lower taxes create jobs.

President	Jobs Created (in millions)	
Jimmy Carter	10.345	4 years
Ronald Reagan	16.131	8 years
George HW Bush	2.637	4 years
Bill Clinton	22.891	8 years
George W Bush	1.281	8 years
Barack Obama	8.677*[9]	81 mos.

Table 8

---

[8] Bureau of Labor Statistics (BLS.gov). Note that the month of inauguration (January) data is assigned to the outgoing president.

[9] Obama's total begins in February 2009. The total is from February 2009 - October 2015. The 4.292 million jobs lost from February 2009 - December 2009 are factored into Obama's totals.

NOTE: As inauguration dates are in late January every 4 years, calculations for total jobs created for each President begin February 1st of inauguration year and end January 31st of the following inauguration year.

The averages below are through October 2015. As of November 5, 2015, September and October data is still preliminary. The monthly totals below reflect the 4.292 million jobs lost from February 2009 – December 2009.

Average Number Monthly Jobs by President

Another great way to analyze each president's performance on job creation is to do a monthly average analysis. This shows an "apples vs. apples" analysis, since some presidents served four years while others served eight years.

President	Average Per Month
Jimmy Carter	215,521
Ronald Reagan	168,031
George HW Bush	54,938
Bill Clinton	238,448
George W Bush	13,344
Barack Obama	107,123[10]

Table 9

The average monthly jobs created from January 2010 through October 2015 is 185,271 (70 month period).[11]

Total Number of Jobs by Party

Once again, this will be one of those charts that is just a dagger in the heart of those Republicans who claim that their party is the party of "job growth."

---

[10] Bureau of Labor Statistics. (BLS.gov); as of November 5, 2015, from February 2009 through October 2015

[11] BLS.gov. September and October 2015 preliminary data pending.

> ➤ Of particular interest about this chart is its span of nearly 4 decades.

> ➤ One would think that if a party's political platform were credible, certainly over the course of nearly 40 years, it would have been consistently dominant in its results.

Even when you factor in the 4.292 million jobs lost from February to December 2009, in the midst of the Great Recession, jobs created while Democrats occupied the White House are *still more than double* the number of jobs created by Republicans in the White House since 1977 (even though Republicans have maintained the White House for a longer period).

Democrats	Jobs	Republicans	Jobs
Jimmy Carter	10.345	Ronald Reagan	16.131
Bill Clinton	22.891	George HW Bush	2.637
Barack Obama	8.677[12]	George W Bush	1.281
Totals	41.913		20.049

Table 10

(From January 1977 – October 2015)

---

[12] Bureau of Labor Statistics; BLS.gov. Barack Obama numbers are from February 1st, 2009 through October 2015; September and October 2015 preliminary data pending. As of November 9, 2015.

Job Creation Numbers
Prior to Obama's Presidency

Not trying to be a dead horse here, but it *is* my intent to show in the most dynamic and forceful ways where our country was heading in January 2009, and where it is today.

Month	2008 (thousands)	2009 (thousands)	2010 (thousands)
Jan	15	(796)	32
Feb	(87)	(703)	(68)
Mar	(79)	(824)	161
Apr	(213)	(684)	247
May	(183)	(355)	518
Jun	(172)	(467)	(130)
Jul	(210)	(325)	(64)
Aug	(259)	(217)	(39)
Sep	(452)	(227)	(49)
Oct	(476)	(201)	248
Nov	(765)	(6)	121
Dec	(696)	(283)	89
Totals (millions)	**(3,577)**	**(5,088)**[13]	**1,066**

Table 11

---

[13] The difference between the 5.088 million jobs total figure for 2009 and the 4.292 million jobs total in other tables or text depicting 2009 is due to the fact that the 796,000 jobs lost in January 2009 is attributed to George W Bush, as he was in office until January 20, 2009.

Jobs by Year, by President[14]

Totals are taken from BLS.gov and are current as of October 2, 2015.

Barack Obama

Year	Created (Lost) *(in millions)*
2009	(4.292)[15]
2010	1.066
2011	2.080
2012	2.257
2013	2.388
2014	3.116
2015	2.062[16]
2016	
2017 (Jan)	

Table 12

➢ **Net 8.677 million jobs to date**
   (February 2009 through October 2015)

➢ **12.969 million jobs**
   (January 2010 through October 2015)

➢ **107,123 monthly average**
   (February 2009 through October 2015)

➢ **Absent 2009 - 185,271 monthly average**
   (from January 2010 through October 2015)

---

[14] BLS.gov, as of October 2, 2015.
[15] February 2009 through December 2009.
[16] January 2015 through October 2015. Current data as of November 9, 2015. However, this data may be adjusted slightly, as September and October 2015 data is still considered preliminary data.

<u>George W Bush</u>

Year	Created (Lost) (in millions)
2001	(1.708)
2002	(.507)
2003	.105
2004	2.032
2005	2.506
2006	2.087
2007	1.139
2008	(3.577)
2009 (Jan)	(.796)

Table 13

➢ **1.281 million jobs total**
(February 2001 through January 2009)

➢ **56,000 jobs created under first term**
(February 2001 through January 2005)

➢ **1.225 million jobs created under second term**
(February 2005 through January 2009)

➢ **13,344 monthly average (8 years)**

Bill Clinton

Year	Created (Lost) *(in millions)*
1993	2.506
1994	3.851
1995	2.160
1996	2.824
1997	3.408
1998	3.047
1999	3.177
2000	1.945
2001 (Jan)	(.027)

Table 14

➢ **22.891 million jobs total**

➢ **11.576 million jobs created under first term** *(February 1993 through January 1997)*

➢ **11.315 million jobs created under second term** *(February 1997 through January 2001)*

➢ **238,448 monthly average (8 years)**

George HW Bush

Year	Created (Lost) *(in Millions)*
1989	1.681
1990	0.311
1991	(0.836)
1992	1.171
1993 (Jan)	.310

Table 15

- **2.637 million jobs total**
  (February 1989 through January 1993)

- **54,938 monthly average (4 years)**

Ronald Reagan

Year	Created (Lost) *(in millions)*
1981	(.144)
1982	(2.124)
1983	3.458
1984	3.880
1985	2.502
1986	1.902
1987	3.153
1988	3.242
1989 (Jan)	.262

Table 16

➢ **16.131 million jobs total**
➢ **5.336 million jobs created under first term**
   (February 1981 through January 1985)
➢ **10.795 million jobs created under second term** *(February 1985 through January 1989)*
➢ **168,031 monthly average (8 years)**

Notice the difference in the job market when Reagan's massive 1981 tax cuts were implemented - and what happened <u>after</u> he began raising taxes.

<u>*Jimmy Carter*</u>

Year	Created (Lost) *(in millions)*
1977	3.716
1978	4.265
1979	2.000
1980	.270
1981 (Jan)	.094

Table 17

➤ **10.345 million jobs total**
(February 1977 through January 1981)

➤ **215,521 monthly average (4 years)**

23

Job Creation By Month, by President[17]
(hundreds of thousands; totals in millions)

Barack Obama

	2009	2010	2011	2012	2013
Jan		32	75	380	205
Feb	(703)	(68)	167	247	
Mar	(824)	161	206	216	
Apr	(684)	247	321	87	
May	(355)	518	103	113	
Jun	(467)	(130)	185	35	
Jul	(325)	(64)	117	177	
Aug	(217)	(39)	128	188	
Sep	(227)	(49)	223	144	
Oct	(201)	248	183	213	
Nov	(6)	121	146	164	
Dec	(283)	89	226	293	
Totals	**(4.292)**	**1.066**	**2.080**	**2.257**	**.205**
	2013	2014	2015	2016	2017
Jan		166	201		
Feb	314	188	266		
Mar	115	225	119		
Apr	187	330	187		
May	219	236	260		
Jun	127	286	245		
Jul	164	249	223		
Aug	256	213	153		
Sep	150	250	137 (p)		
Oct	225	221	271 (p)		
Nov	317	423			
Dec	109	329			
Totals	**2.183**	**3.116**	**2.062**		

Table 18

Notice how many years under the Obama economy **exceed the entire number** of jobs created under George W Bush in eight years (1.281 million) and George HW Bush in 4 years (2.637 million).

President[17]   Bureau of Labor Statistics (BLS.gov), as of November 5, 2015

George W Bush

	2001	2002	2003	2004	2005
Jan		(139)	91	160	134
Feb	71	(134)	(151)	46	
Mar	(25)	(20)	(210)	331	
Apr	(282)	(80)	(44)	248	
May	(38)	(8)	(10)	308	
Jun	(131)	56	9	74	
Jul	(112)	(84)	24	33	
Aug	(160)	(16)	(43)	132	
Sep	(241)	(60)	103	162	
Oct	(325)	125	196	345	
Nov	(294)	10	17	64	
Dec	(171)	(157)	123	129	
Totals	**(1.708)**	**(.507)**	**.105**	**2.032**	**.134**
	2005	2006	2007	2008	2009
Jan		277	237	15	(796)
Feb	239	315	88	(87)	
Mar	135	281	188	(79)	
Apr	363	182	78	(213)	
May	176	24	145	(183)	
Jun	243	77	71	(172)	
Jul	375	206	(34)	(210)	
Aug	196	185	(17)	(259)	
Sep	66	156	86	(452)	
Oct	84	3	83	(476)	
Nov	337	209	117	(765)	
Dec	158	172	97	(696)	
Totals	**2.372**	**2.087**	**1.139**	**(3.577)**	**(.796)**

Table 19

Notice the dismal numbers despite lower top marginal tax rates than either Carter, Clinton, or much of Obama's tenure.

Bill Clinton

	1993	1994	1995	1996	1997
Jan		272	326	(19)	235
Feb	242	200	203	431	
Mar	(49)	465	222	267	
Apr	308	349	162	164	
May	267	334	(16)	321	
Jun	181	316	235	288	
Jul	298	378	102	256	
Aug	160	277	248	172	
Sep	239	352	242	225	
Oct	286	213	154	250	
Nov	262	420	149	298	
Dec	312	275	133	171	
Totals	**2.506**	**3.815**	**2.160**	**2.824**	**.235**
	1997	**1998**	**1999**	**2000**	**2001**
Jan		276	125	231	(27)
Feb	303	196	411	130	
Mar	316	151	107	467	
Apr	292	279	376	287	
May	259	406	211	226	
Jun	267	218	261	(47)	
Jul	313	124	319	179	
Aug	(39)	347	166	(15)	
Sep	512	223	214	135	
Oct	341	198	400	(15)	
Nov	306	282	292	225	
Dec	303	347	295	142	
Totals	**3.173**	**3.047**	**3.177**	**1.945**	**(.027)**

Table 20

Notice the numbers despite the 39.6% top marginal rate resulting from the 1993 Deficit Reduction Act. Not only did the job creation numbers improve, but four budget surpluses were attained, in large part, due to the Deficit Reduction Act.

George HW Bush

	1989	1990	1991	1992	1993
Jan		335	(120)	53	310
Feb	258	248	(305)	(63)	
Mar	193	215	(158)	54	
Apr	173	40	(211)	159	
May	118	152	(125)	127	
Jun	116	23	97	67	
Jul	40	(28)	(36)	68	
Aug	49	(221)	6	141	
Sep	250	(88)	32	36	
Oct	111	(159)	16	180	
Nov	277	(150)	(57)	138	
Dec	96	(56)	25	211	
Totals	**1.681**	**.311**	**(.836)**	**1.171**	**.310**

Table 21

Notice the numbers despite a historically low top marginal tax rate of 28%.

Ronald Reagan

	1981	1982	1983	1984	1985
Jan		(326)	224	446	266
Feb	68	(5)	(75)	481	
Mar	105	(130)	172	275	
Apr	73	(280)	276	363	
May	10	(45)	277	308	
Jun	197	(243)	379	379	
Jul	112	(342)	418	313	
Aug	(36)	(158)	(308)	242	
Sep	(87)	(181)	1,115	310	
Oct	(99)	(277)	271	286	
Nov	(209)	(123)	353	349	
Dec	(278)	(14)	356	128	
Totals	**(.144)**	**(2.124)**	**3.458**	**3.880**	**.266**
	1985	1986	1987	1988	1989
Jan		125	172	94	262
Feb	124	107	232	453	
Mar	346	94	249	276	
Apr	196	187	338	245	
May	274	127	226	229	
Jun	146	(94)	172	363	
Jul	190	318	347	222	
Aug	193	114	171	124	
Sep	203	347	228	339	
Oct	188	186	492	268	
Nov	209	186	232	339	
Dec	167	205	294	290	
Totals	**2.236**	**1.902**	**3.153**	**3.242**	**.262**

Table 22

The **Economic Recovery Tax Act of 1981** became law on August 13, 1981 and was hailed as a job creator by supply-sider Republicans. Yet, note what happened after the massive tax cuts were implemented. The **Tax Equity and Fiscal Responsibility Act of 1982** was signed into law on September 3, 1982, which raised taxes.

Jimmy Carter

	1977	1978	1979	1980	1981
Jan		187	137	129	94
Feb	296	353	244	80	
Mar	403	513	426	112	
Apr	338	702	(62)	(144)	
May	360	346	373	(431)	
Jun	399	442	318	(320)	
Jul	348	254	106	(262)	
Aug	238	276	82	260	
Sep	458	137	28	113	
Oct	262	336	157	281	
Nov	379	437	94	257	
Dec	235	282	97	195	
Totals	**3.716**	**4.265**	**2.000**	**.270**	**.094**

Table 23

Notice the numbers despite a 70% top marginal tax rate.

Perspective on the "Jobs" Party

It is hard to imagine how any sane person can actually hold to the notion that lower taxes create jobs, given the overwhelming evidence provided above. Nearly four decades of definitive data is *not* an anomaly. Keep in mind that even with Ronald Reagan's job numbers, his own OMB Director, David Stockman, gave credit to Fed Chairman Paul Volcker's ability to tame inflation as the reason for the Reagan economic turnaround; not as a result of lower taxes as supply-siders continue to believe.

Take a moment to digest the following perspectives as they relate to job creation from 1977 forward.

➢ During **Bill Clinton**'s eight years in office, 22.891 million jobs were created (**Table 10**).

   ○ This was 21.610 million more jobs than were created during George W Bush's eight years in office (1.281 million). (**Table 10**)
   ○ In other words, the number of jobs created under Bill Clinton was 17.87 times the number of jobs created under George W Bush.
   ○ That is 18.973 million more jobs that were created under Bill Clinton than were created under George HW Bush (2.637 million) and George W Bush (1.281 million) **combined**. (**Table 10**)
   ○ In other words, **5.844 times** the number of jobs were created under Bill Clinton than were created under both Bushes **combined** – and, yet, both Bushes had much lower top marginal tax rates than did Bill Clinton.

   Coincidental? I don't think so.

➢ During **Jimmy Carter**'s four years in office, 10.345 million jobs were created (**Table 10**).

   ○ That was 9.064 million more jobs than the 1.281 million jobs that were created during 8 years of George W Bush (**Table 10**).

- ○ That was 7.708 million more jobs than the 2.637 million that were created during 4 years of George HW Bush (**Table 10**).
- ○ That was 6.427 million more jobs that were added during George HW Bush (2.637 million) and George W Bush (1.281 million) combined, over 12 years (**Table 10**).
- ○ That was 3.92 times the number of jobs that were created under George HW Bush.
- ○ That was 8.07 times the number of jobs that were created under George W Bush.
- ○ That was 2.64 times the number added under both Bushes combined, and it was done in just 4 years.
- ○ That was done despite much higher top marginal tax rates.

➤ During Jimmy Carter's four years in office, the monthly average for jobs created was 215,521 (**Table 9** and **Table 23**).
- ○ Under Ronald Reagan's eight years in office, the monthly average was 168,031 (**Table 9** and **Table 22**).
- ○ Under George HW Bush, the monthly average was 54,938 jobs (**Table 9** and **Table 21**).
- ○ Under George W Bush's eight years in office, the average monthly total was 13,344 jobs (**Table 9** and **Table 19**).

Coincidental? I don't think so.

➤ From January 2010 through October 2015, the average monthly job growth under Barack Obama was 107,123, including the 4.292 million job loss from February 2009 to December 2009 (**Table 9**).

- ○ **In 2014 alone**, the Obama economy created nearly three times as many jobs as the George W Bush economy did in 8 years; 3.116 million jobs to 1.281 million jobs (**Table 12** and **Table 10**).

➤ Since 1977, job growth numbers under Democratic administrations have <u>dwarfed</u> those under Republican administrations (**Table 10**).[18]

Coincidental? I don't think so.

---

[18] BLS.gov; September and October 2015 preliminary data pending.

Keith Berkner

Nowhere is the fallacy that lower taxes create jobs, or that the Republican Party is the pro-job growth party, exposed more than it is in Table 10.

It is time that Democrats boldly call out Republicans on their overwhelmingly disproven theories. The next time that a Republican tells you that the GOP is the pro-job growth political party, feel free to show them the love.

You are now up 2-0!

Unemployment Rates

The Bureau of Labor Statistics (BLS) measures the unemployment rate(s) and publishes those updates monthly. Generally, the updates are released at 8:30 am, the first Friday of each month for the preceding month.

Unemployment Rates Inherited

The following Table is provided in an effort to show not only "where we were" when Barack Obama took office, but to serve as a reminder of the historical baselines of the unemployment rates that modern day presidents have inherited from their predecessors, and left to their successors.

U3 Unemployment Rates at Inauguration

President	Rate when Entering Office	Rate when Leaving Office*
Jimmy Carter	7.5	7.5
Ronald Reagan	7.5	5.4
George HW Bush	5.4	7.3
Bill Clinton	7.3	4.2
George W Bush	4.2	7.8
Barack Obama	7.8	5.0[19] See Table 26

Table 24

---

[19] Bureau of Labor Statistics, BLS.gov, as of November 6, 2015.

Ever notice what happens to the unemployment rate when a Bush enters the White House – though lower taxes were either already in place or legislation lowering taxes was passed into law, shortly thereafter?

U6 Unemployment Rates at Inauguration[20]

And for all the talk about what the "real" unemployment rate (U6) is under Barack Obama (9.8% as of October 2015), note what the "real" unemployment rate was when George W Bush entered the White House versus what it was when he left and where it currently stands. (See Table A-15; BLS.gov for future updates.)

President	Rate when Entering Office	Rate when Leaving Office
Jimmy Carter		
Ronald Reagan		
George HW Bush		
Bill Clinton	11.8[21]	7.3
George W Bush	7.3	14.2
Barack Obama	14.2	**See Table 27**

Table 25

For October 2015, the U6 rate was 9.8%.

Lower Taxes Equals Lower Unemployment?

One would think that after lowering the top marginal tax rate to 28% under George HW Bush and lowering the rate to 35% under George W Bush, that the unemployment rates (and job creation numbers) would have been more reflective of the Republican ruse that "lower taxes create jobs."

---

[20] The U6 Unemployment Rate wasn't tracked until January 1994.

[21] Bill Clinton was in office one year before BLS began calculating the U6 rate (1994).

Unemployment Rates Defined[22]

Everyone should have a basic understanding of at least the two unemployment rates sure to come up in virtually any political conversation, as it relates to the job market.

The **"U3" unemployment rate** is the "standard" unemployment rate and is the one most cited. The **"U6" unemployment rate** is more inclusive of subsets of the unemployed and includes those workers working part time (less than 34 hours per week).

****

U1 = Persons unemployed 15 weeks or longer, as a percent of the civilian labor force.

U2 = Job losers and persons who completed temporary jobs, as a percent of the civilian labor force.

U3 = Total unemployed, as a percent of the civilian labor force (official unemployment rate).

U4 = Total unemployed plus discouraged workers, as a percent of the civilian labor force.

U5 = Total unemployed, plus discouraged workers, plus all other persons marginally attached to the labor force, as a percent of the civilian labor force.

U6 = Total unemployed, plus all persons marginally attached to the labor force, plus total employed part time for economic reasons, as a percent of the civilian labor force.

Additional Note: *Persons marginally attached to the labor force are those who currently are neither working nor looking for work but indicate that they want and are available for a job and have looked for work sometime in the past 12 months. Discouraged workers, a subset of the marginally attached, have given a*

---

[22] BLS.gov

job-market related reason for not currently looking for work. Persons employed part time for economic reasons are those who want and are available for full time work but have had to settle for a part time schedule.

Perspective

Though George W Bush inherited a 4.2% unemployment rate from Bill Clinton, he left a 7.8% unemployment rate to Barack Obama (**Table 24**).

In an economy that was losing 796,000 jobs a month (**Table 19**) when Obama took office and 8.665 million jobs between 2008 and 2009 (**Table 11**), Republicans nonetheless lambasted Obama when the unemployment rate stayed above 8%, despite the fact that the unemployment rate had reached 10.0% in October 2009 (**Table 26**), as effects of the Great Recession lingered.

By September 2012, however, that "8% unemployment rate" talking point had fallen flat (**Table 26**), as 4.733 million jobs had by then been added back into the economy (**Table 18** and **Table 12**).

When that happened, Republicans were forced to change their spin. The new spin became focused on the "U6" employment rate, as opposed to the "U3" unemployment rate.

How convenient.

Yet, the U6 rate has actually fallen even further than the U3 rate. From an apex of 17.1% in late 2009 (**Table 27**), it was down to 9.8% by October 2015 – a decrease of 7.3% from its height (**Table 27**). In addition, by October 2015, the U6 was down 4.4% from the day George W Bush left office (**Table 27**).[23]

By comparison, the U3 rate – which peaked at 10.0% in October 2009 (from a 7.8% rate in January 2009) was at 5.0% in October 2015; a drop of 5.0% from its height (**Table 26**) and a drop of 2.8% from when Bush left office.

---

[23] BLS.gov, as of October 15, 2015.

What seems apparent is that Republicans keep changing their standards of measurement. It's obvious that the very last thing they want to do is have an "apples vs apples" comparison. They know they lose if that happens; hence, the ever-changing standards in measurement – from the standard unemployment rate (U3) to the "real" unemployment rate (U6) to the Labor Participation Rate to the number of Americans no longer in the Labor Force.

****

> The U3 unemployment rate was 4.2% when George W Bush took office in January 2001 (**Table 28**). It was 7.8% when he left office 8 years later (**Table 26**). It increased 3.6% during his administration.

> The U3 unemployment rate was 7.8% when Barack Obama took office in January 2009 (**Table 26**). By October 2015, it had dropped to 5.0%, a decrease of 2.8% (**Table 26**).

Can you name the last time a Republican president can say that the U3 unemployment rate decreased 2.8% under his administration? (Hint: It wasn't George W Bush and it wasn't George HW Bush. It wasn't even Reagan.)

****

Even when Republicans turn their focus to the "U6" unemployment rate, the apples versus apples comparison still goes in the Democrats' favor.

> In January 2001, when George W Bush was inaugurated, the U6 unemployment rate was 7.3% (**Table 29**).

> In January 2009, when George W Bush left the White House, the U6 unemployment rate was 14.2% (**Table 27**). Under Bush, the U6 rate increased 6.9%.

When Barack Obama was inaugurated, the U6 unemployment rate was 14.2% (**Table 27**). By late 2009, the U6 rate had risen to 17.1% (**Table 27**), as effects of the Great Recession continued.

> ➢ As of October 2015, the U6 unemployment rate stood at 9.8% (**Table 27**); a decrease of 7.3% from its height in late 2009, and a 4.4% decrease inherited from George W Bush.

Somehow, though, that just goes right critics' heads.

****

Mitt Romney's Promise and GOP Hypocrisy

Remember when Mitt Romney ran for President in 2012 and claimed that, by the end of his first term (ending January 2017), that he would have the unemployment rate down to 6.0%? Republicans were all too happy that Romney could accomplish such a feat in such a short time. Yet, by August 2015, the unemployment rate had reached 5.1% (**Table 26**), and by October 2015, the unemployment rate was at 5.0%. Yet, somehow, Barack Obama still had not done enough.

What would Reagan's U6 Rate Have Been?

One could only imagine what the "real" unemployment rate (U6) would have been from September 1982 through June 1983 when the U3 unemployment rate was 10.1% to 10.8% (**Table 33**), had the Bureau of Labor Statistics been keeping tract of the U6 back then. Would the GOP have been equally as eager to point out the U6 unemployment rate when Ronald Reagan was president?

(You're up 3-0!)

Unemployment Rates, by Month[24]

Barack Obama
(U3) Unemployment Rates by Month

	2009	2010	2011	2012	2013	2014	2015	2016
Jan	7.8	9.7	9.1	8.2	7.9	6.6	5.7	
Feb	8.3	9.8	9.0	8.3	7.7	6.7	5.5	
Mar	8.7	9.9	9.0	8.2	7.5	6.7	5.5	
Apr	9.0	9.9	9.1	8.2	7.5	6.3	5.4	
May	9.4	9.6	9.0	8.2	7.5	6.3	5.5	
Jun	9.5	9.4	9.1	8.2	7.5	6.1	5.3	
Jul	9.5	9.5	9.0	8.2	7.3	6.2	5.3	
Aug	9.6	9.5	9.0	8.1	7.2	6.1	5.1	
Sep	9.8	9.5	9.0	7.8	7.2	5.9	5.1	
Oct	10.0	9.5	8.8	7.8	7.2	5.8	5.0	
Nov	9.9	9.8	8.6	7.8	7.0	5.8	5.0	
Dec	9.9	9.4	8.5	7.9	6.7	5.6		

Table 26

---

[24] Bureau of Labor Statistics, Series ID 11300000, Civilian Labor Participation Rates, Seasonally Adjusted. November 9, 2015

(U6) Unemployment Rates by Month

	2009	2010	2011	2012	2013	2014	2015	2016
Jan	14.2	16.7	16.2	15.2	14.5	12.7	11.3	
Feb	15.2	17.0	16.0	15.0	14.3	12.6	11.0	
Mar	15.8	17.1	15.9	14.5	13.8	12.6	10.9	
Apr	15.9	17.1	16.1	14.6	14.0	12.3	10.8	
May	16.5	16.6	15.8	14.8	13.8	12.1	10.8	
Jun	16.5	16.4	16.1	14.8	14.2	12.0	10.5	
Jul	16.4	16.4	15.9	14.8	13.8	12.2	10.4	
Aug	16.7	16.5	16.1	14.6	13.6	12.0	10.3	
Sep	16.7	16.8	16.3	14.7	13.6	11.7	10.0	
Oct	17.1	16.6	15.8	14.4	13.7	11.5	9.8	
Nov	17.1	16.9	15.5	14.4	13.1	11.4	9.9	
Dec	17.1	16.6	15.2	14.4	13.1	11.2		
CY Jobs	(5.088)	1.066	2.080	2.257	2.388	3.116	See Table 12, Table 18	

Table 27

George W Bush
(U3) Unemployment Rates by Month

	2001	2002	2003	2004	2005	2006	2007	2008
Jan	4.2	5.7	5.8	5.7	5.3	4.7	4.6	5.0
Feb	4.2	5.7	5.9	5.6	5.4	4.8	4.5	4.9
Mar	4.3	5.7	5.9	5.8	5.2	4.7	4.4	5.1
Apr	4.4	5.9	6.0	5.6	5.2	4.7	4.5	5.0
May	4.3	5.8	6.1	5.6	5.1	4.6	4.4	5.4
Jun	4.5	5.8	6.3	5.6	5.0	4.6	4.6	5.6
Jul	4.6	5.8	6.2	5.5	5.0	4.7	4.7	5.8
Aug	4.9	5.7	6.1	5.4	4.9	4.7	4.6	6.1
Sep	5.0	5.7	6.1	5.4	5.0	4.5	4.7	6.1
Oct	5.3	5.7	6.0	5.5	5.0	4.4	4.7	6.5
Nov	5.5	5.9	5.8	5.4	5.0	4.5	4.7	6.8
Dec	5.7	6.0	5.7	5.4	4.9	4.4	5.0	7.3

Table 28

(U6) Unemployment Rates by Month

	2001	2002	2003	2004	2005	2006	2007	2008
Jan	7.3	9.5	10.0	9.9	9.3	8.4	8.4	9.2
Feb	7.4	9.5	10.2	9.7	9.3	8.4	8.2	9.0
Mar	7.1	9.4	10.0	10.0	9.1	8.2	8.0	9.1
Apr	6.9	9.7	10.2	9.6	8.9	8.1	8.2	9.2
May	7.1	9.5	10.1	9.6	8.9	8.2	8.2	9.7
Jun	7.0	9.5	10.3	9.5	9.0	8.4	8.3	10.1
Jul	7.0	9.6	10.3	9.5	8.8	8.5	8.4	10.5
Aug	7.1	9.6	10.1	9.4	8.9	8.4	8.4	10.8
Sep	7.0	9.6	10.4	9.4	9.0	8.0	8.4	11.0
Oct	6.8	9.6	10.2	9.7	8.7	8.2	8.4	11.8
Nov	7.1	9.7	10.0	9.4	8.7	8.1	8.4	12.6
Dec	6.9	9.8	9.8	9.2	8.6	7.9	8.8	13.6
CY Jobs	(1.735)	(.507)	.105	2.032	2.506	2.087	1.139	(3.577)

Table 29

41

Bill Clinton
(U3) Unemployment Rates by Month

	1993	1994	1995	1996	1997	1998	1999	2000
Jan	7.3	6.6	5.6	5.6	5.3	4.6	4.3	4.0
Feb	7.1	6.6	5.4	5.5	5.2	4.6	4.4	4.1
Mar	7.0	6.5	5.4	5.5	5.2	4.7	4.2	4.0
Apr	7.1	6.4	5.8	5.6	5.1	4.3	4.3	3.8
May	7.1	6.1	5.6	5.6	4.9	4.4	4.2	4.0
Jun	7.0	6.1	5.6	5.3	5.0	4.5	4.3	4.0
Jul	6.9	6.1	5.7	5.5	4.9	4.5	4.3	4.0
Aug	6.8	6.0	5.7	5.1	4.8	4.5	4.2	4.1
Sep	6.7	5.9	5.6	5.2	4.9	4.6	4.2	3.9
Oct	6.8	5.8	5.5	5.2	4.7	4.5	4.1	3.9
Nov	6.6	5.8	5.6	5.4	4.6	4.4	4.1	3.9
Dec	6.5	5.5	5.6	5.4	4.7	4.4	4.0	3.9

Table 30

(U6) Unemployment Rates by Month

	1993	1994	1995	1996	1997	1998	1999	2000
Jan		11.8	10.2	9.8	9.4	8.4	7.7	7.1
Feb		11.4	9.9	10.0	9.4	8.4	7.7	7.2
Mar		11.4	9.9	9.8	9.1	8.4	7.6	7.1
Apr		11.2	10.0	9.9	9.2	7.9	7.6	6.9
May		10.8	10.0	9.7	8.8	7.9	7.4	7.1
Jun		10.9	10.1	9.6	8.8	8.0	7.5	7.0
Jul		10.7	10.1	9.7	8.6	8.1	7.5	7.0
Aug		10.5	10.0	9.3	8.6	7.9	7.3	7.1
Sep		10.4	10.1	9.4	8.7	7.9	7.4	7.0
Oct		10.3	9.9	9.4	8.4	7.8	7.2	6.8
Nov		10.1	10.0	9.3	8.3	7.6	7.1	7.1
Dec		10.0	10.0	9.5	8.4	7.6	7.1	6.9
CY Jobs	2.816	3.851	2.160	2.824	3.408	3.047	3.177	1.945

Table 31

Note: The U6 rate wasn't tracked by BLS until January 1994.

George HW Bush
(U3) Unemployment Rates by Month

	1989	1990	1991	1992
Jan	5.4	5.4	6.4	7.3
Feb	5.2	5.3	6.6	7.4
Mar	5.0	5.2	6.8	7.4
Apr	5.2	5.4	6.7	7.4
May	5.2	5.4	6.9	7.6
Jun	5.3	5.2	6.9	7.8
Jul	5.2	5.5	6.8	7.7
Aug	5.2	5.7	6.9	7.6
Sep	5.3	5.9	6.9	7.6
Oct	5.3	5.9	7.0	7.3
Nov	5.4	6.2	7.0	7.4
Dec	5.4	6.3	7.3	7.4
CY Jobs	1.943	.311	(.836)	1.171

Table 32

Ronald Reagan
(U3) Unemployment Rates by Month

	1981	1982	1983	1984	1985	1986	1987	1988
Jan	7.5	8.6	10.4	8.0	7.3	6.7	6.6	5.7
Feb	7.4	8.9	10.4	7.8	7.2	7.2	6.6	5.7
Mar	7.4	9.0	10.3	7.8	7.2	7.2	6.6	5.7
Apr	7.2	9.3	10.2	7.7	7.3	7.1	6.3	5.4
May	7.5	9.4	10.1	7.4	7.2	7.2	6.3	5.6
Jun	7.5	9.6	10.1	7.2	7.4	7.2	6.2	5.4
Jul	7.2	9.8	9.4	7.5	7.4	7.0	6.1	5.4
Aug	7.4	9.8	9.5	7.5	7.1	6.9	6.0	5.6
Sep	7.6	10.1	9.2	7.3	7.1	7.0	5.9	5.4
Oct	7.9	10.4	8.8	7.4	7.1	7.0	6.0	5.4
Nov	8.3	10.8	8.5	7.2	7.0	6.9	5.8	5.3
Dec	8.5	10.8	8.3	7.3	7.0	6.6	5.7	5.3
CY Jobs	(.050)	(2.124)	3.458	3.880	2.502	1.902	3.153	3.242

Table 33

Jimmy Carter
(U3) Unemployment Rates by Month

	1977	1978	1979	1980
Jan	7.5	6.4	5.9	6.3
Feb	7.6	6.3	5.9	6.3
Mar	7.4	6.3	5.8	6.3
Apr	7.2	6.1	5.8	6.9
May	7.0	6.0	5.6	7.5
Jun	7.2	5.9	5.7	7.6
Jul	6.9	6.2	5.7	7.8
Aug	7.0	5.9	6.0	7.7
Sep	6.8	6.0	5.9	7.5
Oct	6.8	5.8	6.0	7.5
Nov	6.8	5.9	5.9	7.5
Dec	6.4	6.0	6.0	7.2
CY Jobs	3.960	4.265	2.000	.270

Table 34

Labor Participation Rates

Nothing – and I mean nothing - is as revealing to the critics' destitute attempts to downplay Obama's job creation numbers and reduced unemployment numbers, as it is when Republicans divert talk to the Labor Participation Rate (LPR). Once again, this is a conversation that every Democrat on God's green earth should wet their pants to be engaged in.

What Is the Labor Participation Rate?

The Labor Participation Rate (LPR) is the "percentage of the population, 16 years and older, that is either employed or unemployed (that is either working or actively seeking work).[25]

Some Background Here

Until September 2012, the GOP never really talked much about the Labor Participation Rate. As mentioned earlier, most of the GOP rhetoric seemed to involve the (U3) unemployment rate, which was still over 8% until that time (**Table 26**).

It was only after the U3 unemployment rate fell below 8% did they find it necessary to change their party's talking points, as it related to the job market.

**Nothing is as meaningless as the
Labor Participation Rate.**

One of the ways in doing this was to divert focus away from the U3 Rate and begin to draw focus and rhetoric toward the Labor Participation Rate;

---

[25] BLS.gov

much in the same way that their focus shifted away from the U3 rate to the U6 unemployment rate.

Get Ready for "Checkmate"

When Republicans steer you to a conversation about the LPR, be sure to let them speak long enough about the LPR so that their own words come back to haunt them. Let them remind you that the LPR (62.4% in September 2015) is at its lowest since the 1977 and 1978 timeframes. It is part of the GOP's talking points. Simply smile and nod your head in agreement.

Then you ask the $100 million question.

Would you prefer a LPR of 64.6 % - 66.2% - as it was in 2008 and 2009 (when our economy lost 8.665 million jobs) – or would you prefer a LPR of 62.4% (October 2015) when our economy has added nearly 13 million jobs, from January 2010 to October 2015? (**Table 35** and **Table 36**)

When you ask the question, sit back and *be ready to grin from ear to ear* **as the fallacy of their point about the LPR begins to sink in. If you're quiet enough, you can probably hear the crickets chirp.**

I think you're up 4-0 now!

Year	Labor Participation Rate for the Year	Number of Jobs Created (Lost)	Unemployment Rate for the Year
1977	61.6 – 62.8	3.960	6.4 – 7.5
1978	62.7 – 63.6	4.265	5.8 – 6.4
1979	63.6 – 63.9	2.000	5.6 – 6.0
2008	65.8 – 66.2	(3.575)	4.9 – 7.3
2009	64.6 – 65.8	(5.088)	7.8 -10.0
2013	62.8 – 63.6	2.388	6.7 – 7.9
2014	62.7 – 63.2	3.116	5.6 – 6.6
2015	**See Table 36**	**See Table 12**	**See Table 26**

Table 35

Historical Labor Participation Rates[26]

- The average rate since 1950 is 63.01%.

- The highest rate since 1950 is 67.30% (January 2000).

- The lowest rate since 1950 is 58.10% (December 1954).

- "Geographics" affect the Labor Participation Rates

    o Size of the Labor Force

    o Retirements – particularly baby boomers

    o Students – both high school and college

---

[26] TradingEconomics.com

Labor Participation Rates
By President, by Month

(And the Number of Jobs Created that Year)

Labor Participation Rates
(Barack Obama)

	2009	2010	2011	2012	2013	2014	2015
Jan	65.7	64.8	64.2	63.7	63.6	63.0	62.9
Feb	65.8	64.9	64.2	63.9	63.5	63.0	62.8
Mar	65.6	64.9	64.2	63.8	63.3	63.2	62.7
Apr	65.7	65.2	64.2	63.7	63.4	62.8	62.8
May	65.7	64.9	64.2	63.8	63.4	62.8	62.9
Jun	65.7	64.6	64.0	63.8	63.5	62.8	62.6
Jul	65.5	64.6	64.0	63.7	63.4	62.9	62.6
Aug	65.4	64.7	64.1	63.5	63.2	62.8	62.6
Sep	65.1	64.6	64.2	63.6	63.2	62.7	62.4
Oct	65.0	64.4	64.1	63.7	62.8	62.8	62.4
Nov	65.0	64.6	64.1	63.6	63.0	62.8	62.5
Dec	64.6	64.3	64.0	63.6	62.8	62.7	
# Jobs	(5.088)	1.066	2.080	2.257	2.388	3.116	See Table 12, Table 18

Table 36

Labor Participation Rates
(George W Bush)

	2001	2002	2003	2004	2005	2006	2007	2008
Jan	67.2	66.5	66.4	66.1	65.8	66.0	66.4	66.2
Feb	67.1	66.8	66.4	66.0	65.9	66.1	66.3	66.0
Mar	67.2	66.6	66.3	66.0	65.9	66.2	66.2	66.1
Apr	66.9	66.7	66.4	65.9	66.1	66.1	65.9	65.9
May	66.7	66.7	66.4	66.0	66.1	66.1	66.0	66.1
Jun	66.7	66.6	66.5	66.1	66.1	66.2	66.0	66.1
Jul	66.8	66.5	66.2	66.1	66.1	66.1	66.0	66.1
Aug	66.5	66.6	66.1	66.0	66.2	66.2	65.8	66.1
Sep	66.8	66.7	66.1	65.8	66.1	66.1	66.0	66.0
Oct	66.7	66.6	66.1	65.9	66.1	66.2	65.8	66.0
Nov	66.7	66.4	66.1	66.0	66.0	66.3	66.0	65.9
Dec	66.7	66.3	65.9	65.9	66.0	66.4	66.0	65.8
# Jobs	(1.735)	(.507)	.105	2.032	2.506	2.087	1.139	(3.377)

Table 37

Labor Participation Rates
(Bill Clinton)

	1993	1994	1995	1996	1997	1998	1999	2000
Jan	66.2	66.6	66.8	66.4	67.0	67.1	67.2	67.3
Feb	66.2	66.6	66.8	66.6	66.9	67.1	67.2	67.3
Mar	66.2	66.5	66.7	66.6	67.1	67.1	67.0	67.3
Apr	66.1	66.5	66.9	66.7	67.1	67.0	67.1	67.3
May	66.4	66.6	66.5	66.7	67.1	67.0	67.1	67.1
Jun	66.5	66.4	66.5	66.7	67.1	67.0	67.1	67.1
Jul	66.4	66.4	66.6	66.9	67.2	67.0	67.1	66.9
Aug	66.4	66.6	66.6	66.7	67.2	67.0	67.0	66.9
Sep	66.2	66.6	66.6	66.9	67.1	67.2	67.0	66.9
Oct	66.3	66.7	66.6	67.0	67.1	67.2	67.0	66.8
Nov	66.3	66.7	66.5	67.0	67.2	67.1	67.1	66.9
Dec	66.4	66.7	66.4	67.0	67.2	67.2	67.1	67.0
# Jobs	2.506	3.851	2.160	2.824	3.408	3.047	3.477	1.945

Table 38

Labor Participation Rates
(George HW Bush)

	1989	1990	1991	1992
Jan	66.5	66.8	66.2	66.3
Feb	66.3	66,7	66.2	66.2
Mar	66.3	66.7	66.3	66.4
Apr	66.4	66.6	66.4	66.5
May	66.3	66.6	66.2	66.6
Jun	66.5	66.4	66.2	66.7
Jul	66.5	66.5	66.1	66.7
Aug	66.5	66.5	66.0	66.6
Sep	66.4	66.4	66.2	66.5
Oct	66.5	66.4	66.1	66.2
Nov	66.6	66.4	66.1	66.3
Dec	66.5	66.4	66.0	66.3
# Jobs	1.943	.311	(.836)	1.171

Table 39

Labor Participation Rates
(Ronald Reagan)

	1981	1982	1983	1984	1985	1986	1987	1988
Jan	63.9	63.7	63.9	63.9	64.7	64.9	65.4	65.8
Feb	63.9	63.8	63.8	64.1	64.7	65.0	65.5	65.9
Mar	64.1	63.8	63.7	64.1	64.9	65.1	65.5	65.7
Apr	64.2	63.9	63.8	64.3	64.9	65.1	65.4	65.8
May	64.3	64.2	63.7	64.5	64.8	65.2	65.7	65.7
Jun	63.7	63.9	64.3	64.6	64.6	65.4	65.5	65.8
Jul	63.8	64.0	64.1	64.6	64.7	65.4	65.6	65.9
Aug	63.8	64.1	64.3	64.4	64.6	65.3	65.7	66.1
Sep	63.5	64.1	64.3	64.4	64.9	65.4	65.5	65.9
Oct	63.8	64.1	64.0	64.4	65.0	65.4	65.7	66.0
Nov	63.9	64.2	64.1	64.5	64.9	65.4	65.7	66.2
Dec	63.6	64.1	64.1	64.6	65.0	65.3	65.7	66.1
# Jobs	(.050)	(2.124)	3.458	3.880	2.520	1.902	3.153	3.242

Table 40

Labor Participation Rates
(Jimmy Carter)

	1977	1978	1979	1980
Jan	61.6	62.8	63.6	64.0
Feb	61.9	62.7	63.8	64.0
Mar	62.0	62.8	63.8	63.7
Apr	62.1	63.0	63.5	63.8
May	62.2	63.1	63.3	63.9
Jun	62.4	63.3	63.5	63.7
Jul	62.1	63.2	63.6	63.8
Aug	62.3	63.2	63.6	63.7
Sep	62.3	63.3	63.8	63.6
Oct	62.4	63.3	63.7	63.7
Nov	62.8	63.5	63.7	63.8
Dec	62.7	63.6	63.9	63.6
# Jobs	3.960	4.265	2.000	.270

Table 41

What's the Moral to this Story?

When Republicans point to the Labor Participation Rate (and tell you that it hovers around 1977 or 1978 levels), remind them that in 1977 and 1978, our economy added 8.225 million jobs (**Table 23** and **Table 41**).

To show them how silly talk of the LPR is, in trying to characterize a job market, <u>once again ask the question</u>.

Would you prefer a LPR of 64.6 % - 66.2% (as it was in 2008 and 2009) when our economy lost 8.665 million jobs, or a LPR of 62.4% (September 2015 LPR) when our economy added nearly 13 million jobs, from January 2010 to October 2015? (**Table 12**, **Table 18**, **Table 36** and **Table 37**).

Trump: 93 Million "Want to Work"

In an interview with Time on August 18, 2015, 2016 Republican presidential candidate Donald Trump stated, "We have a real unemployment rate that's probably 21%. It's not 6. It's not 5.2 and 5.5. Our real unemployment rate – in fact, I saw a chart the other day, our real unemployment rate – because you have ninety million that aren't working. Ninety-three million to be exact. If you start adding it up, our real unemployment rate is 42%. We have a lot of people who want to work." [27]

Then, during his speech on September 28, 2015 to unveil his tax plan, Donald Trump again used the 93 million figure in addressing unemployment, but in this instant, he went a step further with his wording, when he said, "We have 93 million people in this country that are in serious trouble that _want to work_, that can't work."

In using the phrases that he used, and conveying the message that 93 million Americans were in "serious trouble" and "want to work," but can't work, Trump significantly overstated his case. Specifically, his statement that 93 million people "want to work" is demonstrably false, according to the Bureau of Labor Statistics (**Table 42**). [28]

While the Bureau of Labor Statistics data for August 2015 clearly indicated 93.706 million Americans were not in the labor force (Table A-16; BLS. gov), the same Table also indicated that only 5.920 million of that number "currently want a job." That is less than 6.4% of the 93 million figure that Trump seems to convey that "want a job." (**Table 42**)

---

[27] Time interview with Editor Nancy Gibbs, Washington Bureau Chief Michael Scherer, and political correspondent Zeke Miller.

[28] Table A-16, BLS.gov as of September 28, 2015.

Partial content of Table A-16 (BLS) for August 2015 data

Category	Total	
	Aug 2014	**Aug 2015**
NOT IN THE LABOR FORCE		
Total not in the Labor Force	91,794	93,706
Persons who currently want a job	6,382	5,920
Marginally attached to the labor force	2,141	1,812
Discouraged workers	775	624
Other persons marginally attached to the labor force	1,366	1,188
MULTIPLE JOBHOLDERS		
Total multiple jobholders	6,819	6,901
Percent of Total Employed	4.7	4.6
Primary job FT, secondary PT	3,658	3,832
Primary and secondary both PT	1,748	1,708
Primary and secondary jobs both FT	269	286
Hours vary on primary or secondary job	1,085	1,038

Table 42

Since Trump's statement, the September 2015 data has been released. Per the BLS, the number not in the labor force has increased to 94.718 million; yet, interestingly, only 5.584 million *"currently want a job,"* reflecting that only 5.9% of the 94.718 million not in the labor force 'currently want a job **(Table 43)."**[29]

---

[29] Table A-16, BLS.gov as of October 10, 2015.

**Partial content of Table A-16 (BLS)
for September 2015 data**

Category	Total	
	Sep 2014	Sep 2015
NOT IN THE LABOR FORCE		
Total not in the Labor Force	92,543	94,718
Persons who currently want a job	6,007	5,584
Marginally attached to the labor force	2,226	1,912
Discouraged workers	698	635
Other persons marginally attached to the labor force	1,527	1,287
MULTIPLE JOBHOLDERS		
Total multiple jobholders	7,100	7,297
Percent of Total Employed	4.8	4.9
Primary job FT, secondary PT	3,785	3,859
Primary and secondary both PT	1,926	1,999
Primary and secondary jobs both FT	252	267
Hours vary on primary or secondary job	1,103	1,109

Table 43

In addition, in an interview with Sarah Palin on August 28, 2015, Trump claimed, "they look for jobs, they give up, and all of a sudden, statistically, they're considered employed." This statement, too, flies in the face of reality and is not how employment and unemployment numbers are calculated. In short, if people have given up seeking employment, they are counted as either "unemployed" or "not in the labor force," not as "employed."

So What's Wrong with Trump's Claim?

In conveying the notion that "93 million" Americans "*want to work*," but "can't work," Trump is omitting some rather significant variables.

According to Politifact.com, of the 93 million-plus people who are not currently in the labor force, as of July 2015:[30]

- 9.7 million high school students, age 16-19 years old

- 4.3 million students, age 20-24

- 1.4 million students, age 25-29

- 771,000 students, age 30-34

- 10.3 million stay at home moms

- 2.0 million stay at home dads

- 9.0 million receiving disability checks

- 745,000 in job training, age 24-29

In addition, for the August data, **Table A-6** (BLS.gov) indicated that there were 24.025 million persons with a disability not in the labor force.[31] Granted, a portion of the categories may overlap, but the numbers in each category make Trump's claim, verifiably, statistically impossible.

Politifact.com also notes what many others intuitively understand. Of the 93 million (now higher) out of the labor force, many people "aren't likely looking for work. In addition to the categories listed above, those out of the workforce even include "trust-fund kids who are living off investments."[32]

Certainly, Gary Burthess, an economist with the Brookings Institute, the also takes issue with the notion that 93 million persons are involuntarily out of the labor force and "want a job," as Trump has conveyed.

Burthess notes that there are 8.3 million officially unemployed, another 6.4 million who want a job but haven't looked for a job recently ("discouraged

---

[30] Politifact.com; "Donald Trump says U.S. has 93 million people 'out of work' but that's way too high;" August 31, 2015.

[31] BLS.gov, Table A-6, September 29, 2015.

[32] Politifact.com, 28 September 2015.

workers") and yet another 6.5 million who are working part-time for noneconomic reasons (those involuntary part-time workers who would prefer to be working full-time).[33]

According to Burthess, *even if* all three of these categories were added together, that would still be just over 21 million people, and that total would still be *less than one-fourth* of the 93 million total that Trump claimed during his tax plan speech who "wanted a job."

Note: The number not in the labor force was 94.718 million in September 2015 and will continue to rise as baby boomers continue to retire.

This should make it 5-0.

---

[33] Politifact.com; "Donald Trump says U.S. has 93 million people 'out of work,' but that's way too high," August 31, 2015.

Budget Deficits

In 2012, Bloomberg Politics Poll conducted a survey and found that only 6% of the public knew that the deficit was getting smaller, while 62% said that the deficit was increasing.[34]

In late 2014, Bloomberg Politics Poll again conducted a survey and found that 73% thought that the deficit was getting bigger and only 21% thought that the deficit had gotten smaller, while 6% were unsure.[35]

According to Paul Krugman of the New York Times, in early 2014, only 19% of Americans who took part in a recent political survey knew that deficits had actually *decreased* under Barack Obama.[36]

In short, to hear many tell it, the deficit has skyrocketed under Barack Obama.

Why do folks not understand this?

First, many Americans simply don't know the difference between the budget deficit and the national debt. Though related, they are entirely different.

---

[34] MSNBC.com; "The public has no idea the deficit is shrinking," Steve Benen, December 9, 2014.
[35] MSNBC.com; "The public has no idea the deficit is shrinking," Steve Benen, December 9, 2014.
[36] The New York Times; Paul Krugman. "Secret Deficit Lovers," October 9, 2014; citing a YouGov poll earlier in the year.

A budget *deficit* is the difference between tax revenues for a given fiscal year (October 1 - September 30) and government expenditures (spending) for that fiscal year.

The *national debt* is the cumulative amount of annual deficits (and the interest borrowed to finance debt).

Second, let's face it. When it comes to learning political truths, Americans are lazy. It is the reason why hundreds of millions of dollars are spent to confuse voters and to 'spin' the message.

This is yet another reason why I wrote "Politicuffs."

Third, Republicans do everything they can to convince folks that Barack Obama's "**spending**" has kept deficits high, not only in absolute dollars, but as a percentage of GDP. In reality, nothing is further from the truth (**Table 44**).

As stated previously, FY 2009 was George W Bush's final fiscal year. Why is this important? It is important because it shows the spending baselines that Obama inherited. Spending for FY 2009 was $3.517 trillion (**Table 45**).

As **Table 44** below indicates, spending under Barack Obama remained relatively flat from Bush's FY 2009 level of $3.517 trillion (**Table 45**), to Obama's sixth fiscal year (FY 2015) level of $3.677 trillion – an increase of around $160 billion from FY 2009 levels; or 4.5% over the 6-year period.

Barack Obama Receipts and Outlays[37]

Fiscal Year	Receipts (billions)	Outlays (billions)	(Deficit) in billions
2010	2,162.706	3,457,079	(1,294.373)
2011	2,303.466	3,603,059	(1,299.593)
2012	2,450.164	3,537,127	(1,086.963)
2013	2,775.103	3,454,605	(679.505)
2014	3,021.000	3,504,000	(483.000)
2015	3,251.000	3,677,000	(426.000)
2016			
2017			

Table 44

In comparison, George W Bush increased spending **88.8%** over Clinton's final fiscal year baseline expenditures of FY 2001. Spending went from $1.863 trillion in FY 2001 to $3.517 trillion in FY 2009 (**Table 45** and **Table 46**).

George W Bush Receipts and Outlays

Fiscal Year	Receipts (billions)	Outlays (billions)	(Deficit) in billions
2002	1,853.136	2,010.894	(157.758)
2003	1,782.314	2,159.899	(377.585)
2004	1,880.114	2,292.841	(412.727)
2005	2,153.611	2,471.957	(318.346)
2006	2,406.869	2,655.050	(248.181)
2007	2,567.985	2,728.686	(160.701)
2008	2,523.991	2,982.544	(458.553)
2009	2,104.989	3,517.677	(1,412.688)

Table 45

---

[37] OMB.gov as of 5 October 2015; Treasury.gov as of 15 October 2015. All charts on Receipts and Outlays taken from this source.

Bill Clinton's Receipts and Outlays

FY	Receipts (billions)	Outlays (billions)	+ / -
1994	1,258.566	1,461.753	-203.186
1995	1,351.790	1,515.742	-163.952
1996	1,453.053	1,560.484	-107.431
1997	1,579.232	1,601.116	-21.884
1998	1,721.728	1,652.458	69.270
1999	1,827.452	1,701.842	125.610
2000	2,025.191	1,788.950	236.241
2001	1,991.082	1,862.846	128.236

Table 46

Through FY 2014, spending under Obama had actually *decreased* from the FY 2009 level – George W Bush's final fiscal year - from $3.517 trillion (**Table 45**) to $3.504 trillion (**Table 44**).

Let that sink in for a moment.

So, what's the moral to this story?

The moral to the story is that while spending under Obama remained relatively flat from the FY 2009 baseline of $3.517 trillion (**Table 45**), the deficit has been reduced close to 70% as of the end of FY 2015 (**Table 44**).

This Should Beg the Question

*How then was the deficit reduced from $1.412 trillion in FY 200 (**Table 45**), if spending was not significantly decreased since then (**Table 45** and **Table 44**)?*

The deficit reduction from FY 2009 levels ($1.412 trillion) to FY 2015 levels ($426 billion) was a primary result of increased tax revenues (**Table 45** and **Table 44**).

As the Tables indicate, tax receipts increased $1.146 trillion from FY 2009 (**Table 45**) to FY 2015 (**Table 44**). The *primary* factor in the huge $986 billion deficit decrease was revenue increases – not spending reductions.

In other words, given that the increase in tax revenues from FY 2009 to FY 2015 ($1.146 trillion) outpaced the $986 billion decrease in deficit baselines from FY 2009 to FY 2015, one could argue that the entire 70% reduction in deficits from FY 2009 to FY 2015 was solely attributed to increases in tax revenues.

So what lesson does this tell us?

It tells us that though federal spending has remained flat, tax receipts have drastically increased since FY 2009. It tells us that the Republicans' characterization on Obama's spending as it relates to deficits is misleading. It is worth repeating. The $1.146 trillion increase in tax revenues from FY 2009 baselines more than covers the $986 billion in deficit reduction from FY 2009 to FY 2015.

Also Noteworthy

It is also noteworthy for those (John Kyl and Mitch McConnell) who would have you believe that tax revenue does not affect deficits to understand the following.[38]

Nearly half (**44%**) of the rise in the deficit from FY 2008 to FY 2009 was a *direct result* of reduced tax revenues in FY 2009. In FY 2008, tax revenues were nearly $2.524 trillion. In FY 2009, revenue had dropped to $2.105 trillion (**Table 45**). The FY 2009 deficit was $1.412 trillion (**Table 45**). Of the $960 billion deficit *increase* from FY 2008 to FY 2009, $419 billion of that amount was *directly related* to a *decrease in tax revenue* from the previous year, by that same amount (**Table 45**)

---

[38] TheAtlantic.com, citing Fox News interview with Senator Kyl and Senator McConnell's subsequent comments to TPMDC's Brian Beutler.

So, what's the message here?

When Republicans tell you that the deficits have decreased because they have curtailed Obama's spending, call them out on this lie. It was not a curtailment of Obama's spending per se, though Obama's spending remained relatively flat over the years from FY 2010 through FY 2015 (**Table 44**).

Rather, the 70% decrease in the budget deficit from FY 2009 to FY 2015 was primarily due to an increase of tax revenues of $1.146 trillion during that same period (**Table 45** and **Table 44**). The FY 2009 deficit was $1.412 trillion (**Table 45**); the FY 2015 deficit was $426 billion (**Table 44**).

6-0!

Other Presidential Receipts and Outlays

(George HW Bush)

FY	Receipts (billions)	Outlays (billions)	+ / -
1990	1,031.958	1,252.994	-221.036
1991	1,054.988	1,324.226	-269.238
1992	1,091.208	1,381.529	-290.321
1993	1,154.335	1,409.386	-255.051

Table 47

(Ronald Reagan)

FY	Receipts (billions)	Outlays (billions)	+ / -
1982	617.766	745.743	-127.977
1983	600.582	808.364	-207.802
1984	666.438	851.805	-185.367
1985	734.037	946.344	-212.308
1986	769.155	990.382	-221.227
1987	854.288	1,004.017	-149.730
1988	909.238	1,064.416	-155.178
1989	991.105	1,143.744	-152.639

Table 48

(Jimmy Carter)

FY	Receipts (billions)	Outlays (billions)	+ / -
1977	355.559	409.218	-53.659
1978	399.561	458.746	-59.185
1979	463.302	504.028	-40.726
1980	517.112	590.941	-73.830
1981	599.272	678.241	-78.968

Table 49

Deficit to GDP Ratios[39]

In an effort to compare deficits to different eras or years, an apples to apples approach is to measure deficits as a percentage of our economy. This is done by measuring the deficit against the size of Gross Domestic Product. The following Table provides that data.

As of Jan 1	Deficit / Surplus (billions)	Deficit / Surplus to GDP Ratio	FY President
1977	(53.659)	-2.57	Ford
1978	(59.185)	-2.51	Carter
1979	(40.726)	-1.55	Carter
1980	(73.830)	-2.58	Carter
1981	(78.968)	-2.46	Carter
1982	(127.977)	-3.83	Reagan
1983	(207.802)	-5.71	Reagan
1984	(185.367)	-4.59	Reagan
1985	(212.308)	-4.88	Reagan
1986	(221.227)	-4.82	Reagan
1987	(149.730)	-3.07	Reagan
1988	(155.178)	-2.95	Reagan
1989	(152.639)	-2.70	Reagan
1990	(221.036)	-3.70	GHW Bush
1991	(269.238)	-4.36	GWH Bush
1992	(280.321)	-4.44	GHW Bush
1993	(255.051)	-3.71	GHW Bush
1994	(203.186)	-2.78	Clinton
1995	(163.952)	-2.14	Clinton
1996	(107,431)	-1.33	Clinton
1997	(21.884)	-0.25	Clinton
1998	69.270	0.76	Clinton
1999	125.610	1.30	Clinton
2000	236.241	2.30	Clinton
2001	128.236	1.21	Clinton

Table 50

---

[39] Research.StLouisFed.org as of October 10, 2015.

Deficit to GDP Ratios

As of Jan 1	Deficit / Surplus (billions)	Deficit / Surplus to GDP Ratio	FY President
2002	(157.758)	-1.44	GW Bush
2003	(377.585)	-3.28	GW Bush
2004	(412.727)	-3.36	GW Bush
2005	(318.346)	-2.43	GW Bush
2006	(248.181)	-1.79	GW Bush
2007	(160.701)	-1.11	GW Bush
2008	(458.553)	-3.12	GW Bush
2009	(1,412.688)	-9.8	GW Bush
2010	(1,294.373)	-8.65	Obama
2011	(1,299.593)	-8.37	Obama
2012	(1,086.903)	-6.73	Obama
2013	(679.505)	-4.08	Obama
2014	(483.000)	-2.8	Obama
2015	(426.000)	-2.4	Obama
2016			Obama
2017			Obama

Table 51

Historically, the Deficit to GDP ratio has been around 3.0%.

National Debt

The first rule of law in discussing debt with anyone is not to allow him or her to tell you what the debt was "when Obama took office." That is the oldest trick in the book. When they frame the debt conversation with the words "when Obama took office," what they are attempting to do is to assign FY 2009 – and the majority of the $1.412 trillion deficit for that year – to Barack Obama, instead of assigning George W Bush's last fiscal year fiasco to – George W Bush.

Usually, they will state, "the debt was $10.8 trillion when he (Obama) took office." In reality, when Obama's first fiscal year began October 1, 2009 (FY 2010), the national debt stood at $11.9 trillion (**Table 52**).

When Obama took office in January 2009, FY 2009 was already four months underway (October 1, 2008). George W Bush's funding and priorities had been well established long before Obama was elected; much less took office. The non-partisan Congressional Budget Office had already projected in early January 2009, at least a $1.2 trillion deficit before Obama was even sworn into office.[40]

Again, as has been mentioned, FY 2009 remains the *elephant in the room* for which nobody wants to be held accountable. Fortunately, reality dictates accountability, and the FY 2009 buck stops on George W Bush's desk.

Assigning blame for the remainder of FY 2009 by using the phrase of what debt was the day Obama took office is no different than George W Bush trying to take credit for Bill Clinton's last budget surplus in FY 2001. And he never even attempted to do that!

Sorry; no cigar.

---

[40] CBO projected deficit of $1.2 trillion in January 2009.

Debt at the Start of Administrations' Fiscal Years

(billions of dollars)

President	Fiscal Years	Debt at FY Start (billions)	% Increase
Carter	1978 – 1981	698.840	42.8%
Reagan	1982 – 1989	997.855	186.4%
GHWB	1990 – 1993	2,857.431	54.2%
Clinton	1994 – 2001	4,406.340	31.8%
GWB	2002 – 2009	5,806.151	105.12%
Obama	2010 – 2015*	11,920.519	

Table 52

As of the end of FY 2015 (September 30, 2015), the national debt stood at **$18,150,617,666,484.33** trillion.[41]

Note

When the debt ceiling increased, so did the debt numbers. As a result, debt increased $339 billion on November 2, 2015 to $18,492 trillion. By November 5, 2015, debt stood at **$18.610** trillion, a substantial increase from end of FY 2015 numbers aforementioned, but still a substantially lower rate of increase than under the Bush administration's 8 fiscal years (105.12%).

Debt When George W Bush's First FY (2002) Began – October 1, 2001

When George W Bush first fiscal year began, the national debt stood at $5,806,151,389,190.21[42] - but for practical purposes, let's just call it $5.8 trillion (**Table 52**).

---

[41] TreasuryDirect.com; "Debt to the Penny," November 5, 2015
[42] TreasuryDirect.com; "Debt to the Penny," October 5, 2015.

Debt When George W Bush's Last FY (2009) Ended – September 30, 2009

At the end of Bush's last fiscal year, the national debt was $11,909,829,003.511.75[43] - but for practical purposes, let's just call it $11.9 trillion (**Table 52**).

Debt Increase Under Bush's 8 Fiscal Years

The $6,103,677,614,321.54 debt increase under President Bush reflects a whopping 105.12% increase in debt over his 8 fiscal years (**Table 52**).

****

These numbers may be verified by using an online search engine and entering "National Debt to the Penny," and going to the TreasuryDirect. gov link. The page allows you to adjust the beginning and ending dates by month, day and year.

****

Incredibly, I've even heard some Republicans claim that during President Obama's very first year in office, that he had already increased debt more than all other presidents in history, combined.

Considering that during Obama's first fiscal year (FY 2010), there was only $3.457 trillion in government outlays (**Table 44**) and the debt was already $11.9 trillion (**Table 52**) before his first fiscal year even began, that is some pretty magical thinking. It shows just how out of touch some people can become. What is scary is the fact that these people are allowed to vote.

---

[43] TreasuryDirect.com; "Debt to the Penny," October 5, 2015.

Debt When Barack Obama's First FY (2010) Began – October 1, 2009

When Barack Obama's first fiscal year began, the national debt stood at $11,920,519,164,319.42[44] - but for practical purposes, let us just call it $11.920 trillion (**Table 52**).

Debt Through Barack Obama's First 6 Fiscal Years (2015) – September 30, 2015

At the end of Barack Obama's sixth fiscal year, the national debt was $18,150,617,666,484.33 – but for practical purposes, let us just call it $18.151 trillion.[45]

Debt Increase Under Obama's First 6 Fiscal Years

Through 6 fiscal years, the national debt has increased $6,230,098,502,164.91, an increase of 52.3% - 52.4%, depending upon whether your baseline begins on September 30, 2009 or October 1, 2009. *Note: The debt increased $460 billion the first week in November 2015 as a result of lifting the debt-ceiling limit.*

Points to be made about national debt.

- Relative debt increases have gone up <u>less</u> under President Obama than it did under President Bush. Debt during George W Bush's 8 fiscal years increased 105.12% (**Table 52**). Through Barack Obama first six fiscal years, debt increased 52.5% (**Table 52**).[46] With budget deficits now at around 2.4% of GDP (**Table 51**), the rate of debt growth should slow, both in terms of absolute dollars

---

[44] TreasuryDirect.gov, "Debt to the Penny." Notice there was nearly $11 billion difference in debt from September 30, 2009 to October 1, 2009.

[45] TreasuryDIrector.gov' "Debt to the Penny." As reflected on October 12, 2015.

[46] TreasuryDirect.gov. Debt increased approximately $460 billion the first week in November 2015 when the debt ceiling was lifted. See Note below Table 52.

and in terms of a percent of GDP, as the size of our economy continues to expand.

- When Republicans try to blame the increase of debt on "Obama's spending," this is a great opportunity to once again point out the relatively flat spending under Obama (**Table 44**) – only 4.5% from FY 2009 baselines (**Table 45**) through FY 2015. Meanwhile, George W Bush increased spending 88.8% during his 8 fiscal years (**Table 45**) from Clinton's FY 2001 baselines (**Table 46**).

- It seems odd that Republicans attempt to convey that Obama has a 'spending' problem, on one hand, when trying to justify **their** budget plans - yet claim that they have curtailed Obama's spending, on the other hand, in an attempt to claim credit for the massive decrease in deficits.

- Yet, the decrease in deficits from the FY 2009 baseline of $1.412 trillion (**Table 45**) to $426 billion in FY 2015 (**Table 44**) is overwhelmingly due to increased tax revenues of $1.146 trillion from the FY 2009 baseline of $2.105 trillion (**Table 45**) to $3.251 trillion in FY 2015 (**Table 44**).

- Obviously, when deficits are drastically reduced, debt accumulates at a much slower pace, relatively speaking.

Tax Receipts and Spending Relative to GDP[47]

(1977-2001)

Tax Receipts to GDP and Spending to GDP percentages provide an "apples to apples" look at taxes and government outlays, relative to the size of our economy in any given year; realizing, of course, that taxes and spending affect national debt.

Year	% Receipts to GDP	% Spending to GDP	FY President
1977	17.5	20.2	Ford
1978	17.5	20.1	Carter
1979	18.0	19.6	Carter
1980	18.5	21.1	Carter
1981	19.1	21.6	Carter
1982	18.6	22.5	Reagan
1983	17.0	22.8	Reagan
1984	16.9	21.5	Reagan
1985	17.2	22.2	Reagan
1986	17.0	21.8	Reagan
1987	17.9	21.0	Reagan
1988	17.6	20.6	Reagan
1989	17.8	20.5	Reagan
1990	17.4	21.2	GHW Bush
1991	17.3	21.7	GHW Bush
1992	17.0	21.5	GHW Bush
1993	17.0	20.7	GHW Bush
1994	17.5	20.3	Clinton
1995	17.8	20.0	Clinton
1996	18.2	19.6	Clinton
1997	18.6	18.9	Clinton
1998	19.2	18.5	Clinton
1999	19.2	17.9	Clinton
2000	20.0	17.6	Clinton
2001	18.8	17.6	Clinton

Table 53

---

[47] Office of Management and Budget: Table 1.2. "Summary of Receipts, Outlays and Surpluses or Deficits (-) as Percentages of GDP: 1930-2020." WhiteHouse. gov, as of October 10, 2015. Treasury.gov as of October 15, 2015.

Tax Receipts and Spending Relative to GDP
(2002-forward)

Year	% Receipts to GDP	% Spending to GDP	FY President
2002	17.0	18.5	GW Bush
2003	15.7	19.1	GW Bush
2004	15.6	19.0	GW Bush
2005	16.7	19.2	GW Bush
2006	17.6	19.4	GW Bush
2007	17.9	19.1	GW Bush
2008	17.1	20.2	GW Bush
2009	14.6	24.4	GW Bush
2010	14.6	23.4	Obama
2011	15.0	23.4	Obama
2012	15.3	22.1	Obama
2013	16.7	20.8	Obama
2014	17.5	20.3	Obama
2015[48]	18.2	20.6	Obama
2016			Obama
2017			Obama

Table 54

One could spend a lot of time poring over this chart and in trying to visualize what an ideal percentage of tax and spending should be, relative to the size of our economy (GDP). I would suggest that, as a starter, one might want to focus on the fiscal years 1998 – 2001 in trying to visualize those ideal numbers, as there were four straight budget surpluses during those years.

---

[48] Congressional Budget Office; Treasury.gov, October 15, 2015.

Short Essays

In case you have yet to notice, "Politicuffs" was written to counter Republican talking points and to provide historical perspective, in a "shut down" fashion – using definitive data from what is widely accepted as the definitive sources.

The following short essays continue that trend, in tone, substance, perspective – and admittedly, at times, in sarcasm.

Ronald Reagan:
A Tax and Spend Liberal

On February 2, 2015, House Speaker John Boehner said, "Today, President Obama laid out a plan for more taxes, more spending and more of the Washington gridlock that has failed middle class families. It may be Groundhog Day, but people can't afford a repeat of the same old top-down policies of the past."[49] Boehner's comments were in response to President Obama's FY 2016 White House budget proposal released earlier in the day.

Said Boehner, "Like the president's previous budgets, this plan never balances – ever. It contains no solutions to address the drivers of our debt, and no plan to fix our entire tax code to help foster growth and create jobs. Worse yet, President Obama would impose new taxes and more spending without a responsible plan to honestly address the big challenges facing our country."

He continued, "While the president's budget is about the past, our budget will be about the future. We will address our government's spending problem and protect our national security. Our budget will balance, and it will help promote job creation and higher wages, not more government bureaucracy."

Now, there are numerous points to be made about Boehner's comments – both in content and in the context in which they were made. Boehner's comments are particularly interesting, given both what he said - and what he did not say.

First, and to reiterate, Speaker Boehner stated that, "Like the president's previous budgets, this plan never balances." To hear Boehner tell it, his party is somehow the party of balanced budgets. To say that the House Speaker was disingenuous in his calls for a balanced budget is quite an understatement, to say the very least.

But to illustrate my point, let us regress for a moment.

---

[49] Speaker.gov; "Speaker Boehner's Statement on President Obama's Budget, February 2, 2015

Bill Clinton passed to George W Bush and a Republican-controlled Congress four straight budget surpluses, from FY 1998 through FY 2001.[50]

- FY 1998 - $ 69.270 billion

- FY 1999 - $125.610 billion

- FY 2000 - $236.241 billion

- FY 2001 - $128.236 billion

Yet, in George W Bush's very <u>first</u> fiscal year (FY 2002), the budget surpluses disappeared. In fact, during Bush's 8 fiscal years, not a single budget was anywhere close to being balanced, much less one having a surplus – and the first 6 years of Bush's administration, he had a Republican-controlled Congress.

Even more telling is the fact that the Republican president left his successor a $1.412 trillion deficit in FY 2009 in a budget that obviously was not balanced! For Boehner to exhibit new concern over budget deficits for Obama's FY 2016 Budget Proposal is amusing to those who are paying attention.

Second, Boehner claimed Obama's budget proposal had "no plan to help foster growth and create jobs." Yet again, his comments lack any sense of reality.

When his party last left the White House, we were in the midst of the worst economy in 70 years and we were in the middle of shedding 8.665 million jobs in 2008 and 2009 (**Table 18** and **Table 19**).[51]

When Boehner made those statements on February 2, 2015, 11.108 million jobs had already been created since January 2010 (**Table 18**) – already more than 8.6 times the number created under 8 years of George W Bush

---

[50] Office of Management and Budget; Table 1.1.5; "Summary of Receipts, Outlays and Surpluses or Deficits (-); 1789-2020; WhiteHouse.gov, October 10, 2015.

[51] BLS.gov; Employment Statistics Survey (National); Series ID: CES 0000000001, Seasonally Adjusted

and more than 4.2 times the number created under four years of George HW Bush.

Yet, somehow, Americans are to believe that Republicans have somehow instantly discovered the way to grow jobs, despite no change in their political philosophy.

Think about that for a moment.

Third, Boehner says that the FY 2016 White House proposal would impose "new taxes and more spending."

Boehner certainly intends to convey to his base an exaggerated degree of government spending and taxation under Obama than the historical record seems to support. Again, given some perspective, this is an interesting and disingenuous spin that John Boehner uses.

- When George W Bush was in office, spending increased **88.8%** during his eight FYs (**Table 45**) from $1.863 trillion in Clinton's FY 2001 baseline (**Table 46**) level to $3.517 trillion under Bush's FY 2009 level.

- Yet, government outlays in Barack Obama's *fifth* fiscal year (FY 2014) were only $3.504 trillion (**Table 44**) – expenditures that were less than George W Bush's five years earlier; $3.517 trillion. (**Table 45**).

- In FY 2015, government spending was still only $3.677 trillion (**Table 44**) – just a 4.5% increase over Bush's baseline spending levels of $3.517 trillion in FY 2009 (**Table 45**).

Fourth, Boehner claims that the GOP proposal would promote "job creation and higher wages."

While the House Speaker's rhetoric on "job creation" has already been discredited based upon the historical data contained herein (**Table 10**), his comments concerning higher wages is also disingenuous.

- It has been the Republican party that has fought against not only job programs (such as the Rebuild America Jobs Act in 2011 and 2012), but the GOP has seemingly done all it could do to suppress wages of American workers by vehemently opposing increases in the minimum wage at every angle.

- Frankly, it's hard to fathom how Boehner can even utter those words – that the GOP plans would promote "job creation and higher wages," given his party's performance and policies over the years.

Finally, it would be of benefit, I believe, to analyze Speaker Boehner's words and his inherent, historical conveyance of Obama as a "tax and spend" president. Boehner's comments concerning the White House FY 2016 Budget Proposal is a clear intent to paint President Obama as a "tax and spend" liberal, as he explicitly calls out government's "spending problem" under Obama's FY 2016 Budget Proposal.

Here's Where it Gets Interesting

According to the St Louis Federal Reserve data (Research.StLouisFed.org), Reagan's Tax to GDP ratio was around 17.67% during his 8 fiscal years. His Spending to GDP ratio was around 21.61% (**Table 53**). Make sure you understand those ratios, for it is spending and taxes relative to the size of the economy (GDP) that provides an "apples to apples" comparison.

Now, does Boehner believe that Ronald Reagan was a "tax and spend" liberal, as well? As the symbolic icon of current-day conservatives, I highly doubt it. But if he *doesn't*, why would he believe that Obama is a tax and spend liberal or why would he try to portray Obama as such? (Otherwise, why else would Boehner use phrases like "new taxes," "more spending," and "like previous budgets" of Obama's in describing the FY 2016 White House Budget Proposal?)

Specifically, the FY 2016 Budget Proposal called for $3.99 trillion in spending, with a $474 billion projected deficit, or 2.5% of GDP. Given the 2.5% deficit to GDP projection, then, GDP is expected to be around $18.960 trillion in FY 2016.

Here's the Kicker

If President Obama's proposed FY 2016 budget was equivalent to Ronald Reagan's average budget outlays of 21.61% of GDP (**Table 53**), Obama's proposed outlays for FY 2016 would actually be $107.256 billion *more* than the $3.99 trillion that he proposed. In other words, if Obama had requested and received 21.61% of the projected FY 2016 $18.960 trillion GDP, the amount requested and authorized would have been $4.097 trillion, instead of the proposed amount of just $3.99 trillion.

While **Reagan's** average <u>tax revenue to GDP</u> was 17.67%, over his eight FYs (**Table 53**): [52]

- Obama's first 6 fiscal years' average tax to GDP has averaged 16.21% (**Table 54**).

****

Think about that the next time that you hear that
Obama is a tax and spend President.

****

While **Reagan's** average <u>spending to GDP</u> was 21.61% over his eight FYs (**Table 53**):

- Obama's first 6 fiscal years spending to GDP has averaged 21.77% (**Table 54**)

****

Think about that the next time that you hear that
Obama is a tax and spend President.

****

Seemingly, by Boehner's own characterization of what a 'tax and spend president" is, then, Ronald Reagan must have certainly been one.

---

[52] St Louis Federal Reserve (Research.StLouisFed.org)

The Clinton Surplus:
What Happened

In August 1993, Bill Clinton signed into law the Budget Deficit Reduction Act, which increased top marginal tax rates on personal income from 31% to 39.6% on incomes over $250,000 a year. (The rate was raised from 28% to 31% the previous year.) [53]

The Budget Deficit Reduction Act passed with no support from Congressional Republicans, as the GOP claimed that the legislation would "kill jobs."[54] Despite those assertions, however, 22.891 million jobs were created under Bill Clinton, from February 1993 through January 2001.[55]

Due in large part to those tax increases on incomes over $250,000 and because of additional tax receipts from the millions of new jobs created over Clinton's tenure, by FY 1998, the U.S. economy realized its first of four straight budget surpluses (FYs 1998-2001).

The surpluses were so great that by the time Bill Clinton left office, the nonpartisan Congressional Budget Office had projected $5.6 trillion in surpluses over the next 10-year period.[56]

The projected surpluses were so great that in his first State of the Union Address, President George W Bush said that he would pay down $2 trillion of the national debt over the next 10 years. When Bush's first fiscal year (FY 2002) began, debt stood at just $5.8 trillion (**Table 52**).[57]

---

[53] TaxPolicyCenter.org.

[54] Politifact.com; "Have Republicans 'never done anything really' to tame the nation's deficit?" January 13, 2012.

[55] BLS.gov.

[56] WashingtonPost.com; "Mitch Daniels' memory lapse on the budget surplus,' Glenn Kessler, March 1, 2011.

[57] TreasuryDirect.gov; Debt to the Penny, 15 October 2015.

So what happened?

First, despite vowing to pay down $2 trillion on the (then) $5.8 trillion debt in his first State of the Union Address, Bush instead changed course and decided *against* that action. Instead, his administration passed two huge tax cuts in 2001 and 2003 at a cost to the U.S. Treasury in the trillions.[58]

Despite George W Bush's assertions during his first State of the Union Address, that his administration would pay down debt $2 trillion over the following 10 years, the administration eventually became convinced that paying down the debt would do the U.S. "great economic harm," as acknowledged by his OMB Director, Mitch Daniels, at the time.[59]

In light of today's GOP hard rhetoric on the size of our national debt, take a deep breath and let that sink in for a while.

Try to imagine the dichotomy – the fact that George W Bush could have easily paid down $2 trillion of the (then) $5.8 trillion debt with the Clinton surplus, but instead added trillions to the debt by passing two huge tax cuts.

Second, government spending increased 88.8% under Bush's fiscal years from $1.863 trillion in FY 2001 (**Table 46**) to $3.517 trillion in FY 2009 (**Table 45**).

Meanwhile, tax receipts increased by a net difference of only $114 billion by FY 2009 (**Table 45**) from FY 2001 levels (**Table 46**), or 5.7% (after peaking in FY 2007).

The cost of George W Bush's Medicare expansion alone was estimated to cost from $400 billion to nearly $1 trillion, despite the fact that it left 40

---

[58] While estimates of the 2001 and 2003 tax cuts vary widely, the TaxPolicyCenter. org stated in October 2004, "Economic Effects of Making the 2001 and 2003 Tax Cuts Permanent, that "if made permanent," the entire 2001 and 2003 tax cuts will increase federal debt by $4.3 trillion in 2014, or by 25% of GDP in that year.

[59] WashingtonPost.com; "Mitch Daniels' memory lapse on the budget surplus,' Glenn Kessler, March 1, 2011

million Americans uninsured, a 14% wasted intermediary premium, and a "donut hole" for seniors to pay.[60]

Bruce Bartlett, Senior Policy Adviser to Ronald Reagan and George HW Bush, states that through 2012, Medicare Part D added $318 billion to the national debt. He also concludes that Medicare Part D will add $852 billion to the debt over the next 10 years.[61]

Two unfunded wars – in Iraq and Afghanistan – also led to a bludgeoning of the CBO – projected 10 year surplus. Neither war came cheaply. Regardless of whether one feels that Iraq was a justifiable undertaking or not, it nonetheless required tremendous government expenditures to execute.

On top of the expensive tax cuts, two wars, and a significant Medicare expansion came the Great Recession. With the recession came increased expenditures for bank bailouts, tax credits for the working middle class, increased unemployment claims, an increase in the number of food stamp expenditures, and other assistance for the nearly 8.665 million people who had lost their jobs in 2008 and 2009.

George W Bush took us from a CBO-projected $5.6 trillion 10 year surplus – to $11.9 trillion in debt on the last day of his final fiscal year, FY 2009 (**Table 52**).

---

[60] CNN.com; "Bush signs landmark Medicare bill into law;" December 8, 2003; estimates the cost at $400 billion.

[61] NYTimes.com; "Medicare Part D: Republican Budget-Busting," Bruce Bartlett, November 18, 2013.

FY 2009:
Explosion of the Federal Deficit
The Elephant in the Room

Throughout most of George W Bush's administration, Republicans told us "deficits don't matter."[62] Nowhere were these claims more discredited than in FY 2009.

Though basic truisms should seem obvious to anyone running a household budget, sadly, many politicians seem comfortable in dismissing the revenue side of the ledger when it comes to not only discussing ways to decrease annual deficits, but in acknowledging the fact that a lack of tax revenues has, verifiably, been a major driver of higher deficits. At no time in recent history has this more evident than in FY 2009.

Tax Revenues Decreased $419 billion

In FY 2008, the US Treasury took in $2.524 trillion in tax revenues (**Table 45**). Though tax receipts were only $44 billion less than in FY 2007, the "trickle down" effects (pardon the expression) of the Great Recession were not realized in its full capacity until the following year, as it related to tax receipts.

In FY 2009, the US Treasury took in $2.105 trillion in tax receipts (**Table 45**), $419 billion *less* than in FY 2008.

Government Spending Increased by $535 Billion

In FY 2007, federal outlays were nearly $2.729 trillion (**Table 45**).

In FY 2008, federal outlays were $2.983 trillion, an increase of $254 billion from FY 2007 (**Table 45**).

In FY 2009, federal outlays increased to nearly $3.518 trillion, $535 billion more than in FY 2008 (**Table 45**).

---

[62] Dick Cheney's comments to Treasury Secretary Paul O'Neill to justify funding Bush programs; November 2002.

FY 2009 Budget Deficit Increased $954 Billion

In FY 2008, the federal deficit was $458.5 billion (**Table 45**).

In FY 2009, the federal deficit was $1.412 trillion – an increase of $954 billion from the previous year (**Table 45**)

Breakdown of the Deficit Increase

Of the $954 billion increase in the FY 2009 deficit from the FY 2008 deficit, $419 billion, or 44%, of the increase was a direct result from reduced tax revenue by that same amount, from FY 2008.

Of the $954 billion increase in the deficit that year, $535 billion, or 56%, was due to increases in government spending, to help combat the effects of the Great Recession.

In other words, of the $954 billion increase in the deficit that year, 44% of that increase was directly attributed to the $419 billion in less tax revenue received than was received in FY 2008.

The moral to the story?

Deficits <u>do</u> matter - - - and taxes <u>do</u> affect deficits.

Nowhere is this more apparent than in FY 2009.

Where is the Right-wing Outrage
Over Netanyahu's Lies?

Israel's Prime Minister Benjamin Netanyahu issued an apology Monday, March 23, 2015, over remarks he made just prior to the Israeli election the week before. In an attempt to scare Israeli conservatives into voting for his Likud party, Netanyahu warned conservative Israeli citizens that Israeli Arabs would be voting in "droves."[63]

Netanyahu clearly intended to use fear tactics by inciting what many would call an attempt to race-bait, but he also explicitly stated that there would be no 2-state solution to the Palestinian issue under his government.[64] This was a complete reversal in official Israeli policy, as Netanyahu had publicly indicated for years, an openness to a 2-state solution to the Palestinian issue.

In Netanyahu's apology, he said, "I know that my comments last week offended some Israeli citizens and offended members of the Israeli Arab community. That was never my intent. I apologize for this."

Yet, despite Netanyahu's apology, clearly his intention *was* obvious - not only in his statement referencing Israeli Arabs coming out "in droves" to vote, but also in his stated position just days before the election that there would be no 2-state solution under his leadership, after years of stating otherwise.

Can you even imagine the outcry from conservatives in America had Barack Obama been caught lying openly, for years, about such an important piece of American foreign policy?

---

[63] CNN.com; "Israel's PM Netanyahu: No Palestinian State on My Watch." March 16, 2015

[64] NewYorkTimes.com, "Netanyahu Apologizes; White House is Unmoved.' March 23, 2015

Food Stamp Growth

When Republicans tell you that more Americans are receiving food stamps than at anytime in modern history, feel free to agree with them. That is a truism.

**They should be proud that
they got something right for a change.**

Remind them, however, that when George W Bush was elected president, he assumed the strongest balance sheet in modern history, with 23 million jobs created under the Clinton administration and four straight budget surpluses (FY 1998 to FY 2001).

And remind them that the number of food stamp recipients was around 17.234 million Americans the month Bush took office. And then remind them that the year that Bush left office, the number of food stamp recipients was around 32.205 million, which represents an increase under Bush of 15 million new food stamp recipients – or roughly a 87% increase.[65]

You also want to mention that, though Barack Obama stepped into office in the midst of the worst economy since the Great Depression, where 8.665 million Americans were losing their jobs (**Table 11**), the number of food stamp recipients increased by roughly 13 million recipients or by approximately 45% by the end of FY 2015.

It's all about Perspective.

---

[65] fns.USDA.gov, Table 2.1

Keith Berkner

Do Lower Taxes
Lead to Job Growth?

Since 1980, one of the basic premises of the GOP has been the belief that lower taxes produce more jobs throughout the economy. Certainly, this premise has been echoed time and again since the 1980 presidential campaign.

Certainly, the notion that lower taxes means greater job growth has remained a constant of the Republican platform and is still touted by Republicans today, despite the fact that the premise doesn't hold up to basic scrutiny.

This is yet another point on which Democrats need to be attacking Republicans. It's past time that the GOP is called out and challenged on what they claim. It is time that our citizens understand this myth from reality.

Jimmy Carter

In January 1977, **Jimmy Carter** was inaugurated president of the United States. Under Carter, the top marginal personal income tax rate was 70%. Yet, the Carter economy produced 10.345 million jobs in just four years (**Table 10**), or an average of 215,521 jobs per month (**Table 9**).

Ronald Reagan

In January 1981, **Ronald Reagan** was inaugurated president of the United States. Following the massive 1981 tax cuts, the top marginal personal income tax rate was cut to 50% by 1982, and by 1988 the top rate was reduced yet again to 28.0%.

Though the Reagan economy added jobs after Reagan drastically increased taxes in 1982, to counter his overblown tax cuts the preceding year (**Table 55**), his economy lost 2.124 million jobs in 1982, after negative job growth the preceding year, as well.

It was not until 1983 (after the Reagan tax *increases*), that the Reagan economy began to add jobs (**Table 55**).

(It is noteworthy that Reagan's own OMB Director, David Stockman, attributes the turnaround in Reagan's economy not to the reduction of the massive 1981 tax cuts which Stockman, himself, oversaw – but to Fed Chairman Paul Volcker's ability to tame inflation.)

Year	Created (Lost)[11] *(in millions)*
1981	(.144)
1982	(2.124)
1983	3.458
1984	3.880
1985	2.502
1986	1.902
1987	3.153
1988	3.242
1989 (Jan)	.262

Table 55[66]

For the record, Reagan increased taxes 6 of his last 7 years in office. Overall, the Reagan economy added 16.131 million jobs in 8 years (**Table 10**) and the monthly average was 168,031 (**Table 9**) – less than the monthly average under Jimmy Carter (215,521) and Bill Clinton (238,448). And if you were to eliminate the effects of the Great Recession in 2009 (4.292 million jobs lost), and calculate the monthly average from January 2010 through October 2015 only, Obama's monthly average would be 185,271 jobs (September and October 2015 job numbers pending).

George HW Bush

In January 1989, **George HW Bush** was inaugurated President. Bush enjoyed the 28% top marginal personal income tax rate until 1991, when it was raised to 31.0%. Yet, despite the very low top rate of 28%, the George

---

[66] Bureau of Labor Statistics. BLS.gov, as of November 9, 2015.

HW Bush economy generated only 2.637 million jobs (**Table 10**) - or an average of 54,938 per month during his four years in office.

Bill Clinton

In January 1993, **Bill Clinton** was inaugurated President. One of his first big pieces of economic legislation was signing the 1993 Deficit Reduction Act into law. The intent of this legislation was to raise America's taxes on the high-income earners to help reduce deficits.

Despite Republicans' claims that the Deficit Reduction Act would "kill jobs," 22.891 million jobs were created under Clinton's presidency (**Table 10**); a monthly average of 238,448 jobs (**Table 9**).

George W Bush

In January 2001, **George W Bush** was inaugurated President. Because of Bush's tax cuts, the tax rate was reduced from 39.6% to 39.1% via the Economic Growth and Tax Relief Reconciliation Act of 2001; under the ruse that tax cuts would create jobs.

In 2002, the rate was reduced again to 38.6%, and in 2003, under the Jobs and Growth Tax Relief Reconciliation Act, the top marginal tax rate was reduced to 35.0%.

Despite the lower rates, however, George W Bush's economy created a paltry 1.281 million jobs over his eight years (**Table 10**), or an average of just 13,344 jobs per month (**Table 9**).

Barack Obama

In January 2009, **Barack Obama** was inaugurated President. Despite the economy losing 796,000 jobs that month (**Table 11**) and 5.088 million in 2009 (Table 11), since January 2010 nearly 13 million jobs were created from January 2010 through October 2015 (**Table 12**). [67]

---

[67] 12.969 million jobs from January 2010 through October 2015, minus the 4.292 million jobs lost from February 2009 through December 2009. September and October 2015 preliminary job numbers pending.

And though certainly not all (or even most) of the gains in job creation came before the top marginal rate increased from 35% to 39.6% under Obama, there has been a marked increase in the number of jobs created per year since that marginal rate increase went into effect, as 3.116 million jobs were created in 2014 alone **(Table 12)**

Abortion:
The GOP Hypocrisy

Since the 1980 presidential campaign, Republicans have somehow proclaimed itself the pro-life party.

Frankly, this is one of the most amazing feats I've ever seen in American politics, given that it was the Republican Party that essentially legalized abortion to begin with.

Follow me here while I regress.

As Governor of California, Ronald Reagan signed legislation legalizing abortion in his state in 1967, 6 years before the Roe vs. Wade decision was decided by the US Supreme Court. Yet, by the 1980 presidential campaign, Reagan was the face of the pro-life movement and of American conservatism.

In 1973, the U.S. Supreme Court made abortion legal in all 50 states in its landmark decision, Roe vs Wade. The decision to legalize abortion was a 7-2 decision. Despite the Republican Party self-identifying as the pro-life party, five of the seven votes in favor of legalizing abortion came from Republican-nominated Supreme Court Justices. (See the following Table.)

Justice	Nominated By	Vote to Legalize Abortion[68]
Warren E Burger*	Richard Nixon	Yes
William O Douglas	Franklin D Roosevelt	Yes
William J Brennan, Jr	Dwight Eisenhower	Yes
Potter Stewart	Dwight Eisenhower	Yes
Thurgood Marshall	Lyndon Johnson	Yes
Byron White	John F Kennedy	No
Harry Blackmun	Richard Nixon	Yes
Lewis F Powell, Jr	Richard Nixon	Yes
William Rehnquist	Richard Nixon	No

Table 56

---

[68] Roe v Wade case in 1973; 7-2 decision

In 1980, Ronald Reagan ran as a staunch pro-life conservative, and is somehow considered the icon of the conservative political movement of the modern era, despite the fact that he, as the Governor of California, legalized abortion in that state in 1967. That was 6 years before Roe vs. Wade made abortion legal in all 50 states.

Three of Five Reagan / Bush Appointees Sided with Pro-Choice Challenge to Roe

Interestingly, after Reagan took office in 1981, he nominated Sandra Day O'Connor and Anthony Kennedy to the U.S. Supreme Court. Despite running as the pro-life candidate in 1980, two of four of Reagan's nominees to the Court voted to keep abortion legal when challenges to Roe vs Wade came before the Court. In 1992, in Planned Parenthood vs. Casey, O'Connor and Kennedy joined David Souter, a George HW Bush appointee to the Court, in declaring that the "holding of Roe vs. Wade should be retained." [69].

Between Reagan and George HW Bush, 5 Justices were placed on the U.S. Supreme Court. Despite conveying a pro-life platform, three of their five nominees voted to keep abortion legal when challenges to Roe came before the Court.[70]

Mitt Romney

In 2012, Mitt Romney miraculously took a page from the Reagan playbook and became a pro-life candidate before he ran for president, despite the fact that he was a staunch pro-choice politician as Governor for the liberal state of Massachusetts.

Question

Doesn't it seem a little strange that Republicans seem to exploit the pro-life voters each election, given the major role they have played in legalizing abortion, both at a state level and at the national level?

---

[69] MSNBC.com; "O'Connor had immense power as swing vote;" July 1, 2005.
[70] Planned Parenthood vs Casey, 1992

The Iran Agreement:
Are We Safer Now?

A highly polarizing issue under Obama has been the P5+1 Agreement (also called the Joint Comprehensive Plan of Action) with Iran. The intent of the agreement, of which the United States, Great Britain, France, Russia, China (P5) and Germany (+1) are a party, is to keep Iran from obtaining a nuclear weapon.

Millions of dollars were spent on lobbying Congress in support of, and in opposition to, the agreement. [71] Republicans even went so far as to invite Israeli Prime Minister Benjamin Netanyahu to address Congress in early 2015 on the dangers of the agreement. Republican Senators, too, sent a letter to the Iranian government in an attempt to undermine the P5+1 agreement.

Certainly, supporters and critics of the Iran agreement, alike, claim that their method of dealing with Iran is the best to keep it from obtaining a nuclear weapon.

Among other things, critics of the agreement call for *further* international sanctions to extract even further concessions from Iran. They object to billons of dollars going to Iran as part of any agreement. Critics point to a history of Iranian proxy wars waged around the world. They also disagree on how inspections will be performed.[72]

So what does the Joint Comprehensive Plan of Action agreement do?[73]

> With this agreement, Iran is forced to give up 98% of its stockpile of enriched uranium. Iran would get to keep 300kg of the 10,000 kg it currently has – enriched at no more than 3.67% (not enough enrichment needed for a weapon) for the next 15 years.[74]

---

[71] NPR.org; "Lobbyists Spending Millions to Sway the Undecided on Iran Deal," Alisa Chang; August 6, 2015.

[72] WSJ.com, "The Iranian Nuclear Inspection Charade," July 15, 2015; William Tobey.

[73] NPR.org; "6 Things You Should Know About the Iran Nuclear Deal," July 14, 2015.

[74] NPR.org; "6 Things You Should Know About the Iran Nuclear Deal," July 14, 2015.

➢ With this agreement, Iran agrees to turn its Fordow facility into a research center where Iranian and world scientists will work together.

➢ With this agreement, the Arak site, the only Iranian facility known to make weapons-grade plutonium, will be rebuilt. It will be rebuilt using an international community-approved design, making any further production of plutonium impossible at that site.

➢ With this agreement, Iran's centrifuge stockpile is reduced to around 6,500 from an estimated 18,000 - 20,000 centrifuges currently on hand. Prior to the agreement, there were about 10,000 centrifuges spinning. Spinning is the centrifuge process required of centrifuges to turn uranium into enriched uranium.[75]

➢ With this agreement, the advanced centrifuges will be eliminated and changes will be made to the spinning speeds of the remaining centrifuges.

➢ With this agreement, members of the International Atomic Energy Agency (IAEA) will be on-site during inspections.

Points About the Agreement

First, while anger about the Iran agreement in the United States has almost solely been waged against President Obama, <u>five other major industrial powers</u> have signed on to the agreement as primary participants.

Second, the United Nations Security Council has unanimously voted to support the P5+1 agreement, 15-0.

Third, violation of the agreement by Iran automatically triggers reapplication of sanctions.

---

[75] CNN.com; "Centrifuges and Secret Sites: Get up to Speed on the Iran Nuclear Talks;" Jeremy Diamond, March 30, 2015. This article estimates the number of centrifuges at around 18,000.

Fourth, the agreement prevents Iran from obtaining a nuclear weapon for a number of years; 10 years minimum.

Fifth, without the agreement, it is doubtful that the international sanctions would have remained in place, as other countries economies have been negatively impacted by the international sanctions.

Sixth, while many critics of the agreement have tried to demonize Obama for his support of the agreement, as a sign of being an enemy of Israel, it is interesting to note that soon after the agreement was announced, a poll showed that 49% of American Jews supported the agreement while only 31% opposed the agreement.[76]

Additionally, a LA Jewish Journal survey found 48% of Jews support the deal while 28% opposed it. This poll found that Jewish support for the agreement was 20% higher than for Americans overall.[77]

To follow the rationale of many critics' of the agreement and of critics of Obama for his support of the agreement, might we assume that American Jews don't understand Israeli Jews or that American Jews are, too, an enemy of Israel?

Finally, while Iran and the U.S. will certainly continue to be at odds in other areas of the world, the agreement does accomplish its main task of keeping a nuclear weapon away from Iran for the near future.

While Republicans have overwhelmingly lambasted Obama over the agreement, the Obama administration countered the criticism by comparing the previous administration's desires over an Iran agreement with its own.[78]

But you are probably not going to hear that from critics of the agreement or from the right-wing media.

---

[76] The Jerusalem Post; "Poll: US Jews more likely to back Iran deal than non-Jews," July 24, 2015.

[77] The Washington Post; "Jewish Americans support the Iran nuclear deal," Scott Clement; July 27, 2015.

[78] Washington Post; Glenn Kessler, "Kerry's Claim that Bush offered Iran 'way beyond' what Obama Negotiated." August 13, 2015.

Keystone XL:
A Jobs Package?

For years, the Keystone XL oil pipeline project was presented as a major jobs program that would bring tens of thousands of direct or indirect jobs to the economy. The plans were for the Keystone XL pipeline to transport Canadian oil from that country to the Gulf Coast, through America's heartland. Keystone XL supporters argued that the project could lead to lower gas prices in the U.S. while critics argued that production of the pipeline would actually cause a surge in the price of oil.[79]

It has been interesting to watch supporters push the pipeline as a major jobs program. Indeed, Keystone's own website touted the production of the pipeline with 9,000 direct jobs, and up to 42,000 direct of indirect jobs overall.[80] House Speaker John Boehner reportedly claimed it could create more than 100,000 jobs.[81]

But the Keystone XL project does not provide tens of thousands of *permanent* jobs as Speaker Boehner and Republicans conveyed.[82] Frankly, absent financial kickbacks for support for the project, it is hard to imagine why anyone would support production of the pipeline for a variety of reasons.

> ➤ While certainly many jobs would be necessary to build the pipeline during the first 2 years of the pipeline construction, the project would add only 35 to 50 permanent jobs to the economy. The CEO of TransCanada, himself, has confirmed this.[83]

---

[79] CBSNews.com; "How would the Keystone pipeline affect U.S. gas prices?" Bruce Kennedy, November 17, 2014.

[80] Keystone-xl.com.

[81] FoxNews.com; "Fellow Democrats press Obama to approve Keystone, following environmental report;" February 1, 2014.

[82] Speaker.gov; "A National Embarrassment." Speaker Boehner's comments on Obama's veto of Keystone Jobs bill.

[83] Politifact.com: "CNN's Van Jones says Keystone pipeline only creates 35 permanent jobs;" February 10, 2014.

> ➢ The oil that would have been transported to the Gulf of Mexico via the pipeline would have been sold on the world's open market and would likely not have reduced oil prices in the U.S.[84]

> ➢ The United States assumes the environmental risks in the event of a pipeline leak.

Yet, despite the facts that the pipeline would only produce 35-50 permanent jobs post-construction period, the U.S. would assume all environment liabilities and cleanup related to a break in the pipeline, and the construction of the pipeline wouldn't reduce the price for U.S. oil, supporters continued to push the construction of Keystone XL as a huge benefit to the economy.

I would submit that if House Speaker John Boehner and his party were truly interested in a jobs creation program, that John Boehner would have allowed a vote on the House floor in late 2011 or 2012 on the Rebuild America Jobs Act – when unemployment was still over 8% and their "8% unemployment" talking point was still intact.

The Rebuild America Jobs Act legislation would have added 1.9 million jobs to the economy, including funding for 650,000 teachers, cops and firefighters that had already been laid off by late 2011, according to the nonpartisan CBO.[85]

The Act also meant up to 2% additional GDP and a full percent further decrease in the unemployment rate.[86] (At the time, GDP was running around $16 trillion, meaning an increase of just over $300 billion to our

---

[84] CBSNews.com; "How would the Keystone pipeline affect U.S. gas prices?" Bruce Kennedy, November 17, 2014.

[85] CBSNews.com; "Obama: No GOP plan creates as many jobs as Jobs Act;" October 13, 2011.

[86] Economic Policy Institute (EPI.org); "Would full passage of Obama's Jobs Act have added another million jobs?;" September 6, 2012. Estimates are 0.5% to 0.7% decrease in unemployment rate and an additional 1.6 million jobs for 2012 alone.

economy.)[87] According to CBO estimates, passage of the Act would have decreased deficits by $3 billion.[88]

One must question the motives for Boehner's refusal to allow even a vote on the House floor of this legislation, given its magnitude. One can only surmise that the Rebuild America Jobs Act had a good chance of passage had he allowed the vote to occur.

But, then again, had Boehner allowed a vote on the Rebuild America Jobs Act in late 2011 and 2012, the 8% unemployment rate would have fallen months sooner than it actually did, and the GOP would have had one less talking point to try and hold on to.

And John Boehner was not about to let that happen, regardless of how much it helped America.

---

[87] BEA.gov.

[88] CBO.gov; Congressional Budget Office Cost Estimate, S.1549, American Jobs Act of 2011.

The 2nd Amendment:
Not an Absolute Right

Nothing – and I mean nothing – seems to disturb a right-wing gun lover, more than bringing up the topic of gun control. Even increased scrutiny at tradeshows with enhanced background checks (despite 90% of Americans who support stricter background checks prior to the purchase of firearms) riles their dander.[89]

I certainly cannot say what is, or is not happening at your house, but I have been quite disappointed that President Obama has not been by to collect my guns.

To hear many gun enthusiasts talk, by now, President Obama should have already confiscated every gun in America. Apparently, he has not fulfilled the expectations of his critics – even after 7 years in office.

Certainly, one would have thought that by now he would have dropped by to pick up our guns. After all, gun confiscation has been such a priority on his list of things to do (sarcasm added free).

My guess is that, unless he maintains his office through martial law past January 20, 2017 and proves the lunatics correct, he had better hurry and use his Herculean qualities, and Santa Claus type abilities, to prove his critics right.

Unfortunately, between the NRA, right-wing talk show hosts, nutty politicians, gun lobbyists and more than just a few alternate-world Texans, misinformation and fear-mongering run rampant, in regard to the 2nd Amendment.

While the vast majority of Americans support increased background checks before gun purchases, right-wing fear-mongers still convey that any

---

[89] WashingtonPost.com, "90 percent of Americans want expanded background checks on guns. Why isn't this a political slam dunk?" Scott Clement, April 3, 2013.

effort for increased scrutiny via background checks, even at trade shows, is an infringement on their 2nd Amendment rights.[90]

Naturally, they point directly to the 2nd Amendment,

What does the 2nd Amendment Say?

It reads, "A well-regulated militia, being necessary to the security of a free State, the right of the people to keep and bear arms, shall not be infringed."

Case Law

In U.S. vs. Miller (1939), the U.S. Supreme Court ruled that because automatic weapons and sawed-off shotguns were not part of ordinary firearms of a militia, they were not protected under the 2nd Amendment of the U.S. Constitution.

However, in 2008, in the 2nd Amendment landmark case, Heller vs. DC, the U.S. Supreme Court ruled that citizens *do* have a right to bear arms. In that decision, however, the Court also ruled that owning a firearm is _not an absolute right_ and that the government _can_ regulate (*prohibit*) certain types of gun ownership.

The Kicker?

While many critics like to point to Barack Obama as the threat to their 2nd Amendment Rights, it is actually the U.S. Supreme Court that poses the threat to individual gun ownership.

What the Court Gives, It Can Take Away

Specifically, Justice Antonin Scalia wrote the majority opinion in Heller vs. DC; the opinion that states that the 2nd Amendment *is _not_ an absolute right* and that the government _can_ regulate certain firearms.[91] Paradoxically,

---

[90] WashingtonPost.com; "90 percent of Americans want expanded background checks on guns. Why isn't this a political slam dunk?;" April 3, 2013.

[91] WashingtonPost.com; "Justices Reject D.C. Ban on Handgun Ownership;" June 27, 2008.

Scalia – who wrote that opinion for the majority – is very arguably the most conservative Justice on the U.S. Supreme Court.

The Irony

If you are a liberal listening to the right-wing propaganda about how Obama is a threat to gun ownership, the fact that archconservative Justice Antonin Scalia wrote the majority opinion in Heller vs. DC should amuse you.

If you are a gun-loving conservative, the fact that archconservative Antonin Scalia, wrote the opinion in Heller (that the 2nd Amendment is not to be interpreted as an absolute right to gun ownership), should make you stop and think about your misguided attempts in believing Barack Obama is the threat to your 2nd Amendment rights.

Classic!

The 14ᵗʰ Amendment:
Understanding It

I love the U.S. Constitution. It's one of the greatest documents that's ever been written. I love the Bill of Rights, in particular. The Bill of Rights consists of the first 10 Amendments to the Constitution. The Bill of Rights are those collective amendments to the Constitution that protect our civil rights.

Yet, those 10 Amendments are not the only Amendments that protect our civil rights. In fact, many civil rights issues are not decided by any of the first 10 Amendments, but rather, by the 14ᵗʰ Amendment.

I love the 14ᵗʰ Amendment not because it protects the rights of free speech, peaceful assembly or religious freedom like the 1ˢᵗ Amendment does, but because it gives *all* Americans those rights, regardless of which state they live in.

I love the 14ᵗʰ Amendment not because it gives citizens the right to bear arms as the 2ⁿᵈ Amendment does, but because of its explicit embodiment of rights <u>for all Americans</u>.

I love the 14ᵗʰ Amendment not because it provides the right to remain silent like the 5ᵗʰ Amendment does, but because it provides that right for all Americans, despite where one may call home.

The 14ᵗʰ Amendment simply reads:

"All persons born or naturalized in the United States and subject to the jurisdiction thereof, are citizens of the United States and of the State wherein they reside. No State shall make or enforce any law which shall abridge the privileges or immunities of citizens of the United States; nor shall any State deprive any person of life, liberty or property, without due process of law; nor deny to any person within its jurisdiction the equal protection of the laws."[92]

---

[92] The U.S. Constitution

Now, let me *restate* that Amendment with <u>emphasis added</u> where emphasis is <u>necessary</u>, to reflect its true meaning.

"ALL persons BORN or naturalized IN the UNITED STATES and subject to the jurisdiction thereof, ARE CITIZENS of the UNITED STATES and of the State wherein they reside. NO State shall MAKE OR ENFORCE ANY law which shall abridge the PRIVILEGES or immunities of the United States; nor shall ANY State DEPRIVE ANY PERSON of life, LIBERTY or property, without due process of law; NOR DENY to ANY person within its jurisdiction the EQUAL PROTECTION of the laws."

Two things jump out at me when I read the 14th Amendment.

With the emphasis added, it seems clear that birthright citizenship is explicit in the language contained therein. With the emphasis added, it also seems clear that rights of **all Americans** are guaranteed in the *explicit* language therein, regardless of a citizen's sexual orientation.

Yet, some 2016 Republican presidential candidates have indicated an open willingness to totally disregard the 14th Amendment and openly call for the deportation of American citizens, who were born in the United States, thereby ignoring explicit language of that document, as it relates to birthright citizenship.

Likewise, a disproportionate number of Republicans seem to believe that gay and lesbian citizens are somehow *not* covered under the Equal Protection Clause of the 14th Amendment, and that the majority of the U.S. Supreme Court

Justices somehow practice "judicial activism" when they dare suggest such. Some have even suggested that the Court's ruling on the equality issue is unconstitutional.

Think about the ramifications of that position for a moment – the position that Justices sitting on the United States Supreme Court are acting in an unconstitutional manner by insuring discrimination against gay and lesbian American citizens is prohibited – that insuring equal protection under the 14th Amendment is somehow "judicial activism" and un-American.

I wonder if the critics are familiar with the terms "judicial review," "checks and balances," – or if they understand the significance of Marbury vs. Madison.

Somehow, I tend to doubt it.

Keith Berkner

The Lunacy of a "Birther"

Let us suppose for a moment that the "Birthers" are right. "Birthers" are those people who believe that President Obama is not really an American citizen and that he was born in Kenya, and not Hawaii. And during the early part of his presidency, he was hiding his birth certificate for this reason. And of course, once he actually did provide his long form birth certificate, it was deemed a fake.

But whether one believes in the authenticity of Obama's birth certificate or not, let us take a step back in time for a little perspective.

Here we go.

For the Birther logic to be accurate, no less than two Hawaiian newspapers would have had to have incredible foresight to publish a Kenyan baby's birth announcement way back in 1962.

Using a conspiracy theory rationale, the newspapers' staffs would have had to believe that one day, this little bi-racial kid from Kenya not only would believe that he could run for the office of President of the United States, but that he could actually win the presidency.

In 1962.

Two years before the Civil Rights Act was even signed into law in the United States.

Reflections for a Moment

Why 2016 Matters

US Supreme Court Justice	Born	Age at Inauguration	Nominated by
Antonin Scalia	3/11/36	80	Reagan
Anthony Kennedy	7/23/36	80	Reagan
Ruth Bader Ginsberg	3/18/33	83	Clinton
Stephen Breyer	8/15/38	78	Clinton

Table 57

Is the GOP really the party of "Smaller Government?"

- Ask them why George W Bush's spending levels increased 88.8% from FY 2001 spending levels (last Clinton budget), despite having a Republican-controlled Congress for the first six years of Bush's presidency.

- Ask them why Ronald Reagan nearly tripled the national debt, from $997 billion (FY 1981 baseline) to $2.8 trillion in FY 1989.

- Ask them why there were 300,000 more federal employees under Ronald Reagan than under Carter, Clinton or Obama.

When Republicans complain about Barack Obama's vacations, ask them where their outrage was when George W Bush and Ronald Reagan were away from the White House.

Vacations[93]

Ronald Reagan	390 days
Bill Clinton	174 days
George W Bush	405 days
Barack Obama	160 days

Table 58

Note: As of December 22, 2014.
(Data is for the same period of time in office.)

As of August 12, 2015, Obama took 33 visits to Camp David for all or part of 84 days, while George W Bush, during the same period in office, took 108 trips for part of, or all of, 341 days.

****

Remember when Barack Obama came off the golf course just in time to witness the execution of Osama bin Laden? Don't you wish every President could play golf like that?

Golf[94]

George W Bush	24 rounds
Dwight Eisenhower	800 rounds (est)
Woodrow Wilson	1,200 rounds (est)
Barack Obama	200 rounds

Table 59

****

---

[93] Mark Knoller, CBS Presidential Factoid Guru, as of December 22, 2014.
[94] Mark Knoller, CBS Presidential Factoid Guru.

And what about when Republicans refer to Barack Obama as "Emporer" or "King Obama" for all those Executive Orders he's signing?

Executive Orders[95]

	EO Numbers	Total EOs
Carter	11967-12286	320
Reagan	12287-12667	381
George HW Bush	12668-12833	166
Bill Clinton	12834-13197	364
George W Bush	13198-13488	291
Barack Obama	13489-13702	214

Table 60

****

And those high gas prices that Republicans warned us about if Obama was re-elected in 2012?

Gas Prices[96]

January 22, 2001	$ 1.511
July 14, 2008	$ 4.164
January 19, 2009	$ 1.898
October 5, 2015	$ 2.277

Table 61

****

And what about those conservatives who were screaming when the unemployment rate was over 8% and Barack Obama was working to get us out of the Great Recession?

---

[95] Archives.gov as of 10 October 2015.

[96] EIA.gov. US Energy Information Agency, as of October 19, 2015. FuelGaugeReport.com posted $2.20 a gallon on October 26, 2015.

Unemployment Rates[97]
(after 1981 tax cuts)

Sep 1982	10.1
Oct 1982	10.4
Nov 1982	10.8
Dec 1982	10.8
Jan 1983	10.4
Feb 1983	10.4
Mar 1983	10.3
Apr 1983	10.2
May 1983	10.1
Jun 1983	10.1

Table 62

(Ronald Reagan was President.)

****

And don't you just love it when Republicans reflect back on the George W Bush years as the good old days?

Dow Jones Industrial Average[98]

January 20, 2009	7,949.09
October 23, 2015	17,646.70

Table 63

---

[97] Bureau of Labor Statistics (BLS.gov), as of October 13, 2015.

[98] Quotes.wsj.com; as of October 15, 2015.

"Who Would Raise Taxes in a Recession?"

Republicans asked in 2009 and 2010.[99]

"Ronald Reagan would"

(David Stockman, Reagan OBM Director, replied, in describing how Ronald Reagan raised taxes 1.2% of GDP in 1982 after unemployment was climbing to over 10% for 10 straight months following Reagan's massive 1981 tax cuts.)

---

[99] Republicans were asking on ABC "This Week," May 1, 2011

*The Declaration of Independence talks about life,
liberty and the "pursuit of happiness."*

The U.S. Constitution does not.

Government Regulations Kill Jobs?

Per Bureau of Labor Statistics, only 0.3% of the jobs lost in 2010 were because of government regulations or government intervention. By comparison, during this time, 25% of those laid off, were laid off because of a drop in business demand.[100]

Economic Policy Institute Data[101]

According to the EPI, "since 2007, about 1.5 million workers a year have lost jobs due to extended mass layoffs. Between 2007 – 2009, about 4,300 a year were unemployed due to extended mass layoffs resulting, according to their employers, from government regulations/interventions."

Furthermore, according to the EPI, the gross average 4,300 who were unemployed due to government regulations or interventions, doesn't take into account any offsetting job creation that the regulations may have spurred."

As a side note, per the EPI, in 2010 alone, "an estimated 160,000 lives were saved by the Clean Air Act Amendments of 1990."

Yet, this is one of the most unchallenged and inaccurate claims in political history.

---

[100] Washington Post.com, "Do Government Regulations Really Kill Jobs? Economists say Overall Effect Minimal;" November 13, 2011.
[101] Economic Policy Institute, (EPI.org), "Regulation, Employment and the Economy," John Irons and Isaac Shapiro, April 12, 2011.

Siena College Project

The Siena College Research Institute, a collection of 238 presidential scholars, has been conducting the US Presidents Study since 1982. Their latest rankings for presidents based upon 20 criteria are as follows.[102]

Rank	President
1	Franklin D Roosevelt
2	Theodore Roosevelt
3	Abraham Lincoln
4	George Washington
5	Thomas Jefferson
6	James Madison
7	James Monroe
8	Woodrow Wilson
9	Harry Truman
10	Dwight D Eisenhower
11	John F Kennedy
12	James K Polk
13	William Clinton
14	Andrew Jackson
15	Barack Obama
16	Lyndon B Johnson
17	John Adams
18	Ronald Reagan
19	John Quincy Adams
20	Grover Cleveland
21	William McKinley
22	George HW Bush
23	Martin Van Buren
24	William Howard Taft
25	Chester Arthur

Table 64

---

[102] USNews.com, "Survey Ranks Obama 15th Best President, Bush Among Worst;" July 2, 2010.

Rank	President
26	Ulysses S Grant
27	James Garfield
28	Gerald Ford
29	Calvin Coolidge
30	Richard Nixon
31	Rutherford B Hayes
32	James Carter
33	Zachary Taylor
34	Benjamin Harrison
35	William Henry Harrison
36	Herbert Hoover
37	John Tyler
38	Millard Filmore
39	George W Bush
40	Franklin Pierce
41	Warren Harding
42	James Buchanan
43	Andrew Johnson

Table 65

Note: There are only 43 rankings given Grover Cleveland was the 22nd and 24th president.

Voices of the Republican Party

Donald Trump

Questions birthright citizenship.

ALL persons BORN or naturalized in the United States, and subject to the jurisdiction thereof, ARE CITIZENS OF THE UNITED STATES and of the State wherein they reside. No State shall make or enforce any law which shall abridge the privileges or immunities of citizens of the United States; nor shall any State deprive any person of life, liberty, or property, without due process of law; nor deny to ANY person within its jurisdiction the EQUAL PROTECTION of the laws.

The 14th Amendment of the U.S. Constitution

Donald Trump

Seems to convey that the Trans-Pacific Partnership was designed so China could come in the backdoor, "as they always do."[103]

China is not a part of the Trans-Pacific Partnership. Trump's assertion was rated "Pants on Fire" by Politifact.[104]

---

[103] Donald Trump during fourth GOP presidential debate, November 10, 2015.

[104] Politifact.com, "Trump says China gets an advantage from the Trans-Pacific Partnership;" November 12, 2015.

Donald Trump

"But if I become president, we're all going to be saying "Merry Christmas" again, that I can tell you.[105]

Happy Holidays, Donald Trump!

---

[105] CBSNews.com. Trump campaign rally, 9 November 2015.

Jeb Bush

*Asks you to name one place where we are better off
than we were 6.5 years ago (late summer 2015)*[106]

(Answer: The United States of America)

	Six and one-half years ago	Today
President	George W Bush	Barack Obama
GDP	-8.2% (4th Qtr 2008)	3.9% (2nd Qtr 2015)
Jobs	Lost 8.665 million	Nearly 13 million created since January 2010
Economy	Worst Recession in 70 years	Solid growth, per Federal Reserve
Deficit	$1.412 trillion 9.8% of GDP (FY 2009)	$426 billion 2.5% of GDP (FY 2015)
Dow Jones Industrial Average	7,949 (Jan 20, 2009)	17,646[107]

Table 66

---

[106] Bush asked this at the 2nd GOP Presidential debate.
[107] As of October 23, 2015

Ben Carson

Muslims apparently do not have a right to become President or hold political office.

"I guess it depends on what that faith is. If it's inconsistent with the values and principles of America, then of course it should matter. But if it fits within the realm of America and consistent with the Constitution, no problem."[108]

But when pressed by CNN if he thought Islam was consistent with the Constitution, he replied, "No, I don't – I do not."

1st Amendment, U.S. Constitution; Freedom of Religion.

---

[108] CNN.com: "U.S. shouldn't elect a Muslim president;" September 21, 2015

Ben Carson

"Obamacare is, really, I think the worst thing that has happened in this nation, since slavery."[109]

<u>Since December 6, 1865 – to Name but a Few</u>

World War 1. 1917-1918.

World War 2. 1941-1945.

Korean War. 1950-1953.

Vietnam. 1965 – 1973.

Lebanon. 1983. 241 Marines dead.

Persian Gulf War. 1990-1991

Iraq. 2003-2013

---

[109] CBSNews.com, "Ben Carson: Obamacare 'worst thing' since slavery;" October 11, 2013. 13th Amendment was ratified December 6, 1865.

Ben Carson

Apparently believes that the Chinese are in Syria, "as well as the Russians."[110] Says his intelligence in Syria is better than Obama's.

---

[110] Ben Carson's closing comments in the fourth GOP debate on Tuesday, November 10, 2015.

Marco Rubio

"If you don't want to vote on things, don't run for office. Be a columnist, get a talk show. Everyone who runs for office knows that what we are called to do here is vote on issues on which sometimes we are uncomfortable."[111]

Says the guy who has one of the worst voting attendance records in the U.S. Senate.[112]

---

[111] Marco Rubio on the Senate floor in April 2015, in reference to Iran agreement amendments.

[112] NBCNews.com, "Rubio Tops the Field in Missed Senate Votes;" October 6, 2015.

Mike Huckabee

Apparently believes that one's 1ˢᵗ Amendment Rights allows A Kentucky County clerk to violate others' 14ᵗʰ Amendment Rights.

John Boehner

"Well, I don't need to see GDP numbers or to listen to economists."[113]

**And therein lies the problem.
If your party doesn't want to see the evidence, how
can it be expected to provide the solution?**

---

[113] Chris Wallace interview with John Boehner on Fox News Sunday, August 1, 2010.

Chris Christie

Says the reason that the New York Times is calling for him to withdraw from the 2016 presidential race is because the New York Times is scared he'll beat Hillary Clinton. Says that the New York Times' call for his withdrawal is nothing more than "liberal bias."[114]

Of course it is.

What other reason could it be?

- It certainly couldn't have anything to do with Christie's 1% support in the polls (October 2015).

- Or the fact that, reportedly, 2/3 of his home state feels abandoned by Christie.

- I'm sure it's ALL because of his (and his one percent's) ability to beat Hillary Clinton, as Christie would have you believe.

---

[114] CNN.com, "New York Times to Chris Christie: Drop Out" Theodore Schleifer, October 30, 2015.

Mitt Romney

Said he would have the unemployment rate down to 6% by the end of his first term, January 2017.[115] His party was thrilled.

By October 2015, the unemployment rate was 5.0%

- *Yet, Barack Obama somehow isn't doing enough?*

- *The GOP would now rather talk about the U6 rate (14.2% when George W Bush left office and 9.8% in October 2015).*

- *The GOP would now rather talk about the Labor Participation Rate.*

- *The GOP would now rather talk about anything but an apples v apples comparison*

---

[115] Mitt Romney on Fox News Fox and Friends.

Mike Lee (Utah)

Suggested that if Barack Obama was re-elected in 2012 that gas prices may go to $6.60 a gallon.[116]

➤ By early December 2014, gas prices were under $2 a gallon in many areas.[117]

➤ As of October 19, 2015, the national average was $2.277, per EIA. gov.

➤ FuelGaugeReport.com reported $2.220 on October 26, 2015.

---

[116] Lee.Senate.gov

[117] Forbes.com; "The Lowest Gas Prices in Every State," December 16, 2014. Ohio locations were selling gas at $1.85 while Louisiana locations were selling gas at $1.86 a gallon.

Newt Gingrich

Suggested that the re-election of Barack Obama might lead gas prices to $10 a gallon.

"If you would like to have a national American energy policy, never again bow to a Saudi king and pay $2.50 a gallon, Newt Gingrich will be your candidate. If you want $10 a gallon gasoline, an anti-energy Secretary, and in weakness requiring us to depend on foreigners for our energy, Barack Obama should be your candidate."[118]

See previous page (and grin).

---

[118] Newt Gingrich on NBCNews.com. February 25, 2012.

Rick Santorum

Wants to abolish the State Department because – well, diplomacy is all they do over there.

"Every problem the State Department has, the answer is diplomacy. Why? Because if it's not diplomacy, they don't have a job."

Moral to the Story?

(Why waste time with diplomacy when we can waste trillions of dollars by engaging the military at every opportunity?)

Final Jabs

Barack Obama's Accomplishments

➢ Inherited an economy contracting at 8.2% in the 4th Quarter 2008. (What is it today?)

➢ Budget deficit reduced by 70% from FY 2009 baseline

➢ From January 2010 through September 2015, 12.686 million jobs created – August and September 2015 preliminary data pending.

➢ Osama bin Laden is dead and the ocean's fish have long since defecated his remains.

➢ General Motors is alive.

➢ Inherited a 7.8% unemployment rate. As of September 2015, the unemployment rate is 5.1%, a decrease of 2.7%. When was the last time a Republican White House could make such claim?

➢ Climate change agreement with China.

➢ The P5+1 agreement to keep Iran from a nuclear weapon.

➢ Opening of relations with Cuba.

➢ 16 million more Americans insured under "Obamacare."

➢ The Rebuild America Jobs Act, which would have added 1.9 million more jobs (most in 2012), added up to 2% GDP and a further decrease of one full percent in the unemployment rate, had Boehner allowed a vote on the House floor.

➢ Lilly Ledbetter Act.

➢ Slashed our oil dependency

Keith Berkner

George W Bush's "Accomplishments"

➢ Inherited one of the strongest balance sheets in U.S. history, yet left the worst recession in 70 years.

➢ Doubled national debt in his 8 fiscal years after vowing to pay down $2 trillion on the national debt with the Clinton surplus, during his first State of the Union address.

➢ Tripled the federal deficit in only 8 fiscal years.

➢ Ignored the 6 August 2001 Intelligence memo warning of an imminent attack on U.S. soil by Osama bin Laden.

➢ 9/11.

➢ Tied Iraq to 9/11 and invaded a country having nothing to do with 9/11

➢ Estimated the cost of the Iraq operation at $60 billion; replaced the White House staffer who dared estimate the cost of Iraq at $150 billion. Miscalculated a minimum of $2 trillion when lifetime veterans' care is factored in.

➢ Most noted response to Katrina: "Good job, Brownie!"

➢ The invasion of Iraq was to last "weeks, 6 months max" according to Dick Cheney.

➢ The $3.2 trillion tax cuts (2001 and 2003) were to act as a stimulus to create jobs. Created the fewest jobs per year of any president since Herbert Hoover.

➢ Over 400,000 innocent Iraqis were killed, and over 4,000 American soldiers lost their lives, in Iraq.

➢ Failed to kill Osama bin Laden.

➢ Installed a pro-Iranian government (al Maliki) in Iraq – yet his party complains about Iranian influence in the region.

138

➢ Inept policies in Iraq led to the rise of ISIS. Released Abu Bakr al-Baghdadi, leader of ISIS, from Camp Bucca, Iraq in 2004.

➢ The Dow Jones Industrial Average was 7949 when he left office. As of October 23, 2015, it was 17,646.

➢ Inherited a 4.3% unemployment rate from Clinton; left Obama a 7.8% unemployment rate.

➢ Expanded Medicare by hundreds of billions of dollars; a plan that left 40 million Americans uninsured, a wasted 14% middleman premium and a donut hole for seniors to pay.

➢ Diverted the world's focus away from Saudi Arabia on 9/11; started a "War on Terror" soon thereafter. Disbanded his core Osama bin Laden team in 2005.

➢ Could not find an "active" Weapons of Mass Destruction program (pre-1992) in Iraq. WMDs found were pre-1992 and presumably ones given to Saddam Hussein by guys with the last names of Reagan and Bush.

➢ Food stamp recipients up 93%, from when he began his administration through the Great Recession.

Ronald Reagan's
"Accomplishments"

➢ Nearly tripled national debt in his 8 fiscal years (from $997 billion to $2.8 trillion).

➢ Iran contra.

➢ 241 Marines killed in Beirut, Lebanon on October 23, 1983 because he felt that Beirut was "vital" to U.S. "interests." Apparently, Lebanon's olive exports were worth the lives of 241 Marines.

➢ Violated the Boland Amendment.

➢ Broke international law in mining Nicaraguan harbors.

➢ Raised taxes 11 times.

➢ CIA trafficked drugs on the backloads of the C-123 aircraft ("The Fat Lady") on contra resupply efforts.

➢ 1981 tax cuts were indeed "voodoo economics" per his own OMB Director, David Stockman. Unemployment rates skyrocketed following 1981 tax cuts.

➢ His tax cuts did not spur the economic recovery as supply-siders like to think, but rather, the Federal Reserve Chairman's ability to "tame inflation," per OMB Director Stockman, in reference to Paul Volcker.

➢ Debt ceiling raised 18 times with no right-wing outrage.

➢ Savings and Loan crisis.

➢ Had the most indictments and convictions of any administration in American history.

Remember This

- Perspective is the Great Equalizer.

- There's Nothing Patriotic About Political Ignorance.

- He who knows the data wins the debate – every time.

- "I don't want to see religious bigotry in any form. It would disturb me if there was a wedding between the religious fundamentalists and the political right. The hard right has no interest in religion except to manipulate it."[119]

- Reverend Billy Graham

[119] Parade, February 1, 1981. Also, cited in "Thy Kingdom Come: How the Religious Right Distorts Faith and Threatens America"

Other BLS Data Tables

The following Tables are from the Bureau of Labor Statistics and are invaluable tools in searching for the latest government data.

Table A-1. Employment status by sex and age.

Table A-2. Employment Status by race, sex and age.

Table A-3. Employment status of Hispanics by sex and age.

Table A-4. Employment status by educational attainment.

Table A-5. Employment status by veteran status, period of service, and sex.

Table A-6. Employment status by disability status, sex and age.

Table A-7. Employment status of the foreign and native born by sex.

Table A-8. Employed persons by class of worker and Part-time status.

Table A-9. Selected employment indicators.

Table A-10. Selected unemployment indicators.

Table A-11. Unemployed persons by reason for unemployment.

Table A-12. Unemployed persons by duration of unemployment.

Table A-13. Employed and unemployed persons by occupation.

Table A-14. Unemployed persons by industry and class of worker.

Table A-15. Alternative Measure of Labor Underutilization.

Note: You'll use this one mainly in discussing the U3 and the U6 unemployment rates.

Table A-16. Persons not in the labor force and multiple jobholders by sex.

Note: You will use Table A-16 a lot when someone tells you, "93 million Americans are out of the workforce."

Update: While showing them that their "93 million" number is close, you can explain the number of those persons who "**currently want a job**" are only 5.584 million (September 2015) – only 5.9% of the 94.718 million out of the workforce in September 2015.

For the record, Table A-16 is "golden" when debating the number of mericans not in the Labor Force.

Printed in the United States
By Bookmasters